A Roadmap to Raising Emotionally Intelligent Children

A Parent's Guide to Ensuring Your Child's Health, Wealth, and Happiness

Elizabeth Benson

information contained within this document, including, but not limited to, errors, omissions, or inaccuracies.

Table of Contents

And a women who held a babe to her breast said "Speak to us of Children" and he answered:

Your children are not your children.

They are the sons and daughters of Life's longing for itself.

They come through you but not from you,

And though they are with you yet they belong not to you.

You may give them your love but not your thoughts,

For they have their own thoughts.

You may house their bodies but not their souls,

For their souls dwell in the house of tomorrow, which you cannot visit, not even in your dreams.

–"On Children," Kahlil Gibran

Introduction

Right now, human beings are the most intelligent living things populating the Earth. At least, that's what most of us would like to believe, if only to avoid doing some serious damage to our self-esteem. Knowing about our own intelligence isn't enough to make the most of it, especially when we consider that there are multiple types of intelligence we possess at once. Like most things, some people will find that their strengths lie in a more traditional, academically-oriented intelligence. Others will find that they tend to be more naturally adept at working with and resolving more emotional matters. Both forms of intelligence and the skills they provide are impressive. However, it seems that we as a society have developed a tendency to place emphasis on the importance of that traditional type, the one we measure with something known as the Intelligence Quotient (IQ).

While academic strength is certainly useful, we have to be considerate of the importance of that second type of intelligence. This one, known as a person's Emotional Quotient (EQ), is essential to a healthy life. By nature, humans are emotional creatures. Our feelings dictate so many of our thoughts, behaviors, and beliefs. To underestimate the importance of emotional intelligence means to set yourself up for failure, as you will be attempting to work and live around a part of yourself that's built into your very being. By understanding this importance, we can teach our children to become more emotionally intelligent. In doing so, we pave a road for them to walk around this difficulty and straight towards happiness and success.

Now, it's one thing to have the distinction between types of intelligence down pat. It's another thing entirely to understand what exactly constitutes IQ and EQ as two distinct, separate concepts of human intelligence. Of the two, you are probably more familiar with the concept of IQ, as the importance of this type of intelligence has been brought up most often through the years. It's also possible that IQ is better known than EQ because the theory of quantifying logical and analytical intelligence has been around longer. The concept of a person's IQ was first introduced to the world in 1883 by Francis Galton, an English statistician. A few decades later, in 1905, the first formal IQ test was constructed by a French psychologist named Alfred Binet. By contrast, EQ has only occupied a space in the popular lexicon since 1985, when Wayne Payne wrote a doctoral thesis centered around the study of human emotion (Diffen, 2019).

People have only begun to examine and focus on EQ in earnest in the last two decades. Naturally, the idea of an EQ, which is a number that represents the level of intelligence held by a person, followed only after the proposal of the existence of a person's Emotional Intelligence (EI). Belief in EI has steadily increased since the 1980s, leading to the creation of the EQ test. In the interest of being comprehensive, it's worth mentioning that EQ is defined as the extent to which a person can express, control, evaluate, and perceive emotions. This ability isn't limited to the person's own emotions but expands to the emotions of those around them as well. By contrast, IQ is described as a person's overall mental ability. This ability is represented by a number, which is obtained through the completion of standardized testing. IQ scores reflect a person's abilities in the fields of critical thinking, logic, and other cognitive processes linked to academic functioning (Cherry, 2013).

It is essential that we understand what IQ and EQ are, respectively, in order to gauge just how multifaceted human intelligence is. However, while this awareness is important, it must be said that when the two are compared side-by-side, it isn't very difficult to see which type of intelligence is likely to carry you further in life. This discussion has expanded much more in recent years as people have come to realize that a person's IQ may not be an accurate or comprehensive representation of their full mental and emotional capabilities. By looking at the power of emotional intelligence, we can teach our children to succeed in all aspects of life.

According to Cherry (2013), the differences between IQ and EQ can be best demonstrated by looking at the different skills with which a high level of each type of intelligence provides a person. Those who score high on standardized IQ tests are likely to be more adept at the following:

- Visual and spatial awareness and the processing of these types of stimuli.

- Understanding the workings of societal structures.

- Fluid reasoning means that their thought process when constructing a solution to a problem is uncomplicated and comes together logically and without difficulty.

- Maintaining the strength of both their working and short-term memories.

- Quantitative reasoning, which may manifest as being skilled at mathematics and problems centered around or involving numbers.

The skills with which a high EQ score imbues a person are much more concerned with the nuances of interpersonal interactions as well as those of an individual's personal development. A high EQ is linked to the following abilities:

- Identifying the emotional state in which the individual, as well as those around them, finds themselves at any given time.

- The deciphering, interpretation, and evaluation of another person's emotions during interactions and when asked for help or advice.

- Maintaining control over their own emotional state, especially when they are undergoing negative experiences and in times of emotional distress.

- Sensing changes in the emotional state of the people around them and knowing how to respond in healthy, constructive ways.

- Building and enhancing interpersonal relationships by expertly maneuvering difficult or new emotional territory.

- Using feelings and expressions of empathy to strengthen their interpersonal bonds.

Naturally, a well-rounded person will exhibit attributes of both types of intelligence. This complexity and coexistence of different types of intelligence within any one person is the whole reason why we are able to determine what our EQ is. Near the end of the 20th century, we began to realize that there is more to being intelligent than just crunching numbers and excelling in academic environments. By itself, life is a complex thing to navigate. Thus, it stands to reason that the mental resources we use to navigate the obstacle course that is the world should be equally sophisticated. That being said, possessing great emotional intelligence is an asset that will take you further in life than you could ever imagine.

The advantages of a high EQ are thought to be so impressive that there are many people who regard this score as more impressive and important than its academic counterpart. This argument is strengthened by the fact that the effects of high emotional intelligence prove beneficial across so many different aspects of a person's life. In recent years, research has demonstrated that the type of intelligence quantified by an IQ score only constitutes roughly 20% of the total intelligence contained within the human mind, as this intelligence relates to success in life (Kadane, 2018). Having a healthy IQ will never be to your detriment, but it won't be all that useful outside the classroom or in situations that require more lateral thinking. We mustn't discard the notion of having academic intelligence. Instead, we should view it as one component of a larger system of intelligence, which is supplemented most prominently by abilities and knowledge related to emotions.

EQ can be used to teach our children about various aspects of life as well as the skills they will need to navigate their futures. When we look at the benefits of a high EQ, the skills we most commonly find are perseverance, motivation, impulse control, the ability to delay gratification, and the ability to develop healthy coping mechanisms (Chancellor, 2022). Over the course of this book, we will explore how these skills can be taught and developed throughout childhood. For now, what we need to realize is that the different types of intelligence we are meant to help our children cultivate don't exist independently of one another. While we should absolutely encourage our kids to read and work with numbers, what will benefit them the most in the long term is understanding the ins and outs of their emotions, as well as those of others, and how to communicate these feelings constructively.

Understanding the importance of this approach is the first step toward raising an emotionally intelligent child. This process can be daunting, as I'm sure you know, given that we are meeting one another within the pages of this book. Achieving your parenting goals isn't always easy, and these difficulties might mean that we feel worry or failure more than success or satisfaction when we look at the way we parent. Our approaches are very much informed by our own lived experiences, and there's no guarantee that these memories will always be pleasant. While drawing from our childhoods can be a good thing, if you are the one hoping to break a multi-generational cycle, your worry will only increase. If you're a first-time parent, you may experience these feelings multiplied by 100.

Though it might sound odd to say, this worry is actually a good thing. Not in life, but simply for the fact that it brought you here and that it motivated you to make a change. Perhaps your experience has been less emotional, and this is why you're here: To ensure that your children have a better, more open, and more expressive emotional life than you do. Some of you will see both of these possibilities and still find your motivation unmentioned. For many of us parents, we are motivated to change aspects of our child-rearing practices because of the things we see happening in our children's lives. We see them struggling to make friends, express their emotional needs, or connect with other people's feelings on a deeper level. There are many things that could have brought you to the pages of this book. The catalyst, while significant, isn't important. The fact that you have followed through is what we must focus on. You will be using this book to build a sustainable approach to emotionally healthy parenting, and this consistency is already a good start.

Describing something as a "sustainable approach" is an incredibly vague description, so we must take a closer look at what exactly your takeaway will be once you have finished this book. At the base level, you will have gained an array of new skills that will help you in your own interpersonal interactions and that will hopefully make you just a little bit more emotionally intelligent as well. However, our greatest focus will be on the ways we can help our kids, and that's what you will gain from this book. By the time you turn the final page, you should have a comprehensive understanding of the field of emotional intelligence. Moreover, you will be able to translate this understanding into a practical approach, one in which you are able to provide your children with a more holistic process of emotional and psychological development. This, in turn, will set them up for the type of success that every parent in the world hopes their child will attain, whatever it may look like.

My hope is that you will achieve all this through reading the contents of this book. For myself, accumulating this knowledge took slightly longer. I spent years tinkering with my parenting approach and never managed to escape that feeling of worry. The same may be true for you now, but it doesn't have to be in the future. Though emotional intelligence is anything but simple, learning how to cultivate it in your children shouldn't be anything but complex. It may not always be as easy as we expect, but it truly is something we can achieve.

If you need something slightly more tangible to cement your belief that you will set your child up for success by enhancing their emotional intelligence, we can turn to some well-known figures to see the benefits of working towards a high EQ. For our purposes here, we'll go with the most popular definition of success, which uses excelling in your career as a metric. There are a number of CEOs who sit at the head of massively influential companies and have attained the top spot through employing the skills and techniques that characterize a high level of emotional intelligence. Indra Nooyi, the former head of PepsiCo; Richard Branson, who founded the Virgin Group; and Satya Nadella, who serves as CEO of Microsoft, are all known for using emotionally intelligent approaches in their work. These leaders of the industry make an effort to connect with their employees, listen to their needs, and effectively communicate the needs and expectations of the company (Morey, 2018). Though you might not define your child's achievement of success as attaining a high-level corporate job, there's no denying that leaning into the emotional side of being human is bound to deliver results.

How you define success and happiness is up to you, but what I can safely assume to be true across the board is that you wish for your child to have both of these experiences in their life. That is the goal of this book—to give you all the tools and knowledge you need to start building an emotionally-healthy future for your child. We've already covered some of the benefits to be gained from improving your emotional intelligence. In addition to these perks, the end goal is to empower your child while simultaneously connecting with them. By the time you finish this book, you will be capable of open and honest communication with your child, both as a recipient and a giver. Ultimately, you will be able to create a safe environment in which your child will learn how to express themselves in a healthy way and which will lend itself to improving other aspects of their life. The hope is that you will be emboldened to make the changes needed to achieve this outcome and, in the process, allow your children to grow alongside you.

On the topic of hope, I would love nothing more than for you to trust me to take you on this journey of discovery and improvement. With a Master's degree in psychology, my published works have led me through a world of research, all of which I share with you here. Through my work, I have been able to gain a deep, profound understanding of human behavior, and will lead you to the right techniques and practices that will change yours for the better. On a more personal level, I have fulfilled the role of nurturer for some time, first for my own children and then for my grandchildren. I've run the gamut of child-rearing and seen the very best methods, the very worst, and everything in between.

When I was going through the process of trial and error, that is, parenting, I would have killed for a book like this. Back then, it was very much a matter of learning as you went. Now, however, I have years of experience, both personal and professional, and can help ease the process of your development into an emotionally intelligent parent. In the process, I can help you raise emotionally intelligent children. I am aware that this may sound boastful, and you'd have every right to be doubtful. However, I ask you to trust me to lead you through this journey, which may very well be the voyage of a lifetime. By the time we reach our destination, you will never again doubt your emotional abilities or those of your child. The learning process won't be easy, but all you have to do for now is take the first step. Don't worry; I'll take it with you, and we'll do it all together.

Chapter 1:

The ABCs of EI

Behind every child who believes in himself is a parent who believed first. —
Matthew Jacobson

Before we can begin to make any changes to our parenting
styles and techniques, it is imperative that we understand
exactly what we are hoping to achieve through these changes.
On face value alone, we can determine that we would like to
raise our children to be more emotionally intelligent. Though
the description of the process is easy enough, getting there
might be more complicated. To make it all the easier on you,
the parent, we'll build our approach from the ground up. And
where else can we start but with foundational knowledge? If we
expect our children to adopt the skills we wish to teach them,
we must first understand the concepts behind these skills and
what they mean for us in everyday life.

What Is Emotional Intelligence?

By now, we have a basic understanding of how we can quantify
a person's emotional intelligence through an EQ. However, this
metric is used in order to understand the depth and breadth of
a person's emotional intelligence (EI), a concept into which we
must delve a little further. Emotions have been factored into
the structure of human behavior for a long time, but the
concept of EI as a separate type of intelligence was first
introduced in the 1990s. Crucially, the presentation of this type

of intelligence described it as an attribute rather than a hindrance, a stance that went against many of the preconceived notions we have about a person's emotionality.

Where EQ is the numerical representation, the EI behind it is described as a person's innate ability to use emotions when communicating. This means that they are able to move through interpersonal interactions and effectively perceive and interpret the emotions of the other person. This perception is followed by the ability to evaluate the appropriate emotional response, demonstrate said response, and control the extent of its severity (Cherry, 2022b).

EI was introduced to the world in 1990 by Peter Salovey and John D. Mayer. They presented the theoretical framework for the definition provided above. The evolved understanding of emotional intelligence we have today comes in large part from the work of Daniel Goleman, who expanded on the work of Salovey and Mayer (Psychology Today, 2019). Through this development, Goleman presented the argument that emotional intelligence and the subsequent EQ score used to describe it were perhaps more important than the academic intelligence quantified by an IQ. Goleman posited that a higher EQ might, in fact, provide a person with a different set of life skills that would put them on an easier and shorter path to success. We will encounter Goleman's work in the field of emotional intelligence a few times throughout the course of this book, so his contributions to our understanding of the concept are definitely worth noting.

The Five Components of Emotional Intelligence

Remember that one Mr. Daniel Goleman we met not five minutes ago? It's time to take a look at one of his most famous expansions of the theory of emotional intelligence. In his 1995 book *Emotional Intelligence: Why It Can Matter More Than IQ*,

Goleman expounds upon the concept of EI as proposed by Salovey and Mayer some five years earlier. His book proposed that EI is actually made up of five different components, each of which provides those with a high score with a particular skill that helps them in their pursuit of success, whatever it may look like:

Self-Awareness

The self-awareness that stems from emotional intelligence involves recognizing and understanding the things you feel and do. This understanding particularly applies to behavioral patterns and their motivations. When you examine your own emotions and actions, you understand what they are, where they come from, and how they affect not only your life but also the lives of those around you.

Being self-aware goes hand-in-hand with regularly monitoring your emotions, recognizing when your emotional state changes, and subsequently being able to describe the emotions contained in this new state. In the process of self-examination, emotionally intelligent individuals are able to draw a line between the things they feel and the behaviors they exhibit. Success ties in with self-awareness through the fact that individuals with this skill understand themselves to a great extent. This means that they are aware of their strengths, weaknesses, and limitations. Subsequently, when they set goals, these parts of their identity are kept in mind. At the same time, they are aware of their capacity for change and will take the opportunity to learn from new experiences and people (Cherry, 2022a).

Self-Regulation

This particular characteristic of a high EQ is somewhat linked to that of self-awareness. Being aware of your emotions is one thing, but exerting control over them is something entirely different. It is essential that we differentiate between emotional control and repression. Self-regulation is very much the former, but it involves feeling what you feel and knowing when the appropriate time is for this emotion. In addition to this, people who are able to self-regulate will very rarely experience emotional outbursts or respond to something disproportionately.

This knowledge and control come along with the skill of impulse control and the delay of gratification. Self-regulation means that a person will work through their emotions in the moment, realize the behavior their feelings will elicit, and accurately determine whether that situation is right for that type of expression (Lebow, 2021). This particular component of a person's EI provides them with skills that help with easing tension during interpersonal altercations, dealing with and resolving conflict, and adapting easily to sudden changes in their environment and plans.

Motivation

The third component of emotional intelligence is characterized by a person's desire for personal development (Lebow, 2021). Motivation involves the setting of goals as well as the adoption of behavioral and emotional patterns that enable a person to achieve what they set out to do. Crucially, the driving force that compels emotionally intelligent people toward action is internal. They don't pursue improvement or change because they want attention, accolades, or external validation. The process is entirely personal and seeks to fulfill that person's emotional needs and desires.

Empathy

Moving on to empathy, we find that this component provides people with the skill of emotional comprehension. This time, however, it isn't their own emotions they have a grasp of, but other people's. Being empathetic means that people with a higher EI are more sensitive to the emotional states of those around them and are able to cope with any sudden changes that may occur in these states. Even if what another person is going through is entirely outside your own frame of reference, strong emotional intelligence means that you can draw on your own version of their experience in order to provide comfort, aid, or advice.

Empathy proves especially effective when it comes to determining power dynamics between people. However, in addition to determining the nature of the dynamic, emotionally intelligent people are able to identify and understand the factors and forces that led to this order of power. As a result, they can navigate the twists and turns of relationships with nebulous power distributions.

Social Skills

The fifth and final component is perhaps the one that comes to mind first when someone mentions a high level of emotional intelligence. Possessing social skills is pretty much what the name suggests: You are able to build lasting, healthy interpersonal relationships. In doing so, individuals with a high EI are often able to learn more about themselves and how their emotions exist in relation to those of other people.

Skills that fall under this umbrella are often those that make people feel at ease during interactions with emotionally intelligent individuals. Examples include eye contact, active listening, open body language, and strong and healthy verbal communication (Lebow, 2021).

Measuring Emotional Intelligence

Naturally, if we understand what constitutes emotional intelligence, we must also understand how exactly it is measured and represented. Tests that measure a person's EI are comprehensive and take into account feelings that present across the entire spectrum of human emotion. Most commonly, EI measurement is divided into three categories: self-reporting, other-reporting, and ability testing (Kellogg, 2022).

Self-Reporting

Much like the name suggests, this method of EI measurement relies on a person's self-perception as well as their understanding of their own emotional state and processes. Self-reporting tests resemble personality tests and allow a person to gain valuable insight into those emotionally intelligent traits they inherently possess. However, this is where we encounter something of a roadblock with self-reporting EI tests. While certainly effective, their accuracy is somewhat contingent on a person having an EI naturally, as this would provide them with the self-awareness to complete the test adequately. That being said, self-reporting tests are an excellent way to gain a basic understanding of your own emotional intelligence. The most popular version of this test is the EQ-i test, developed by Israeli psychologist Reuven Bar-On.

Other-Reporting

Sitting directly opposite self-reporting, we find the method of measuring EI through information relayed by other people. Also known as observer rating (Kellogg, 2022), this approach relies on the person whose EI is the focus of the test being rated and evaluated by those in their life. The idea is that these people will have seen and felt the effects of the test subject's EI, and as such, can accurately gauge how emotionally intelligent the subject is. This methodology presents us with a similar problem as self-reporting. In order to accurately report on the EI of another, a person would have to be fairly emotionally intelligent themselves. If the reporters don't have high levels of EI, it may result in a bias in the test results. However, other reporting is still an effective way of determining how a person is perceived by others in terms of their emotional expression and communication.

Ability Testing

The third and final measurement method is the one most commonly employed and which many believe to be the most comprehensive and conclusive. Ability testing is a form of assessment that focuses on a person's technical skills, which aligns perfectly with the fact that emotional intelligence largely manifests as a specific set of capabilities. There are a variety of EI ability tests, but those used most often measure the different aspects of a person's identity and functioning that highlight their utilization of emotion as well as its recognition and the demonstration of empathy. Popular ability tests include the Multifactor Emotional Intelligence Scale (MEIS) test as well as the Emotional and Social Competence Inventory (ESCI). The latter was developed in part by none other than the godfather of modern EI understanding, Daniel Goleman.

The Signs of High Emotional Intelligence

As we have come to learn, some people are naturally predisposed to those traits and skills that make for an emotionally intelligent person. If we hope to raise emotionally intelligent children, we must first gauge the extent of their innate emotional intelligence (more on that later) and expand upon what is already there. To do so, we can look for certain signs and traits in our children that may be indicative of a naturally high EI level. It is important to note, however, that each person is different. As such, the sections below may describe your child to a T or perhaps only touch on a few aspects of their character. Regardless of how many boxes they check, knowing what to look for now will help you down the line when the time comes to develop their emotional intelligence, however much of it they naturally possess.

Self-Awareness

In early childhood, self-awareness can manifest as any of the following:

- Having the ability to label their emotions as a child is feeling them. Moreover, children are able to differentiate between the nuances of emotions and the subtle differences or resemblances between different feelings.

- Taking ownership of their emotions, both in the moment and in hindsight.

- Understanding what they can and cannot do and taking the initiative to set their own boundaries.

- Having a higher sense of self-esteem and being confident enough to speak up when it is warranted.

- Understanding the difference between self-perception and the view that other people may have of them.

Self-Regulation

In emotionally intelligent young children, the management of their emotions and behaviors may present as any of the following:

- Knowing when it is appropriate to express their emotions and to what extent they should do so depends on the circumstances.

- Having the ability to work through their emotions as they are feeling them and manage the way in which they express their emotions. This particular aspect of self-regulation most often manifests as a child's ability to calm themselves down when upset or to roll with the punches when things suddenly change.

- Avoid impulsive behavior because they consider the consequences or delaying gratification because they understand the concept of greater satisfaction down the line.

- Crying is an extremely important marker of self-regulation. Not only is it a means for a child to communicate with their caregivers, but if children regularly cry, it means that they feel safe to do so. Children with a high level of EI who have had their emotions stifled will be able to discern between spaces in which they can safely express their sadness and those in which they will be chastised for it.

Motivation

When we see motivation in emotionally intelligent children, we see them take action and pursue betterment. This may look like:

- Demonstrating commitment to a goal, desire, or task and seeing it all the way through to the end. This perseverance will endure regardless of whether the end result is positive or negative.

- Having curiosity in spades: Motivation may manifest as a thirst for knowledge and a desire to understand the world so that they can change themselves for the better.

- Learning from mistakes: This goes hand-in-hand with determination and commitment, as emotionally intelligent children will deal with failure as a learning opportunity. They will adjust their approach and achieve success through a process of trial and error.

Empathy

Empathy is one of the traits most associated with emotional intelligence. Empathetic young children may behave in the following ways:

- Relaying the emotional experience of others to their parents, especially if the experience is negative. They will feel the need to communicate someone else's distress because it distresses them as well, and they believe talking about it will help.

- Reaching out to someone they feel may be in some sort of distress because they understand that someone needs a shoulder to cry on or just some support.

- Displaying happiness for others who are happy and feeling genuine delight at someone else's positive experiences.

Social Skills

The fifth and final component of emotional intelligence is perhaps the most overt and can manifest in the following ways:

- Having the ability to actively listen to others during interpersonal interactions. Not only does this allow the other person to feel heard, but it also enables the emotionally intelligent child to gauge the type of reaction the situation warrants and to become genuinely invested in its outcome.

- Knowing that they need to communicate their emotions in order for others to understand what they are going through. Communication surrounding emotions is also a means of forging profound and healthy interpersonal connections.

- Displaying good manners and respect for the structure and proceedings of whichever situation they find themselves in. This extends to being considerate of other people's feelings in shared spaces and making them feel welcome in spaces familiar to the child.

It bears repeating that these are the most common signs and traits attached to high emotional intelligence in early childhood. This list is by no means exhaustive, nor should it serve as a diagnostic tool. If your child does exhibit some of the behaviors discussed here, then it might mean they are naturally emotionally intelligent. This is good news for you, as it establishes a baseline for the development you will undertake with your child. Conversely, if none of the behaviors discussed resemble your child at all, you know that you have a clean slate on which to build the behaviors and characteristics of an emotionally intelligent child.

Why Does Emotional Intelligence Matter?

We have discussed the importance of EI and EQ a few times already, but their significance truly cannot be understated. It is absolutely essential that we help our children develop their emotional intelligence early in life, largely because it will help them gain a better, more comprehensive image of their identity. We've already seen that self-awareness forms part of EI, and while we do facilitate this when helping our children develop emotionally, we are also giving them access to the rich world of feelings that exist within them.

The benefits of cultivating your emotional intelligence stretch far beyond understanding yourself. The more we have come to understand EI, the more we see its effects on so many parts of our lives. Those with a high EQ have been known to score similarly high on tests measuring academic intelligence. The insight and broader perspective brought by a high EQ allow children to excel academically, and they typically do better on standardized tests. In addition to this success in the classroom, emotionally intelligent children tend to have rich social lives and fare well among their peers. They are able to navigate emotional difficulties such as conflict and, in the process, forge deeper, longer-lasting bonds (Morin, 2021).

The importance of emotional intelligence is underscored once more when we consider the fact that, similar to the link between EQ and IQ, a high score of the former can typically be seen as a predictor of success in adulthood. Studies that tracked emotionally intelligent children from ages 5 to 25 demonstrated that they were more likely to obtain degrees through tertiary education and work stable jobs by the age of 25 (Morin, 2021).

Perhaps the most important argument for why we should focus on emotional intelligence is the fact that it has a positive impact on a person's mental health. Children who learn to manage their emotions are able to avoid behaviors that might lead to anxiety or depressive disorders. Moreover, if children know how to communicate openly, they will seek help when in distress and will do so before things become too severe.

How You Can Strengthen Your EI

Naturally, it is important that we work on the strength of our own emotional intelligence as we hope to raise children who will come to have high EI levels of their own. Though we will explore methods of increasing EI throughout the course of this book, what you need to know right now is that there are simple habits you can adopt to begin your own journey of self-improvement.

The best way for you to begin working on your emotional intelligence is to enter into interactions with other people with the intention of actively listening and responding. Allow the other person in the conversation to set the tone and provide emotional cues for you to respond to. Actively listen to what they are saying and how they are communicating their needs or problems. An extension of this practice is becoming more empathetic. This may not come to you naturally or easily, but it will nevertheless improve over time. When you interact with others, and they present you with a problem or tell you of a negative experience, consciously shift your mind to imagine what that might have been like. Put yourself in their shoes by remembering a similar experience from your own past. If you can't do this, continue listening and consider their side of the story and what it must have felt like in the moment.

Finally, you can round out some of your behavioral changes by taking the time to engage in some self-reflection. Whenever you can, revisit the way you expressed your emotions during interactions with others and how you responded to their expressions in turn. Furthermore, take the time to think about your perception of your own emotions. Be honest with yourself and consider how often you allow your emotions to run their course, how often you communicate your feelings to those around you, and to what extent you allow yourself to embrace your own emotionality.

These habits are a small step in the right direction but are by no means enough to constitute a comprehensive, lasting change. That being said, starting small with habits like these will make the bigger steps waiting down the line seem smaller and, subsequently, easier to take.

Practical Exercise

We conclude this chapter with an interactive exercise you can perform. Below, you will find a rudimentary questionnaire you can use to gauge the level of emotional intelligence at which your child is currently operating. Similar to the signs and traits outlined earlier in this chapter, the answers to these questions will provide you with a starting point from which to begin this developmental journey.

This exercise involves only yourself and resembles an other-reporting EI test. You will be asked to recall your child's behaviors as they relate to emotional expression and management. Feel free to write down your answers to the following questions:

1. How does your child respond to sudden changes in their environment, such as quick switches to new tasks?

2. When your child has set a goal or expressed their desire for a particular outcome, how often do they engage in behaviors that will provide them with the desired result?

3. If your child is unsuccessful in achieving a goal or if things don't work out as they had hoped, what is their emotional response?

4. Does your child share their emotions with you, whether prompted to do so or not? Furthermore, is this expression general and vague, or are they able to lend some specifics to the description of their emotional state?

5. When your child speaks about themselves, their thoughts, feelings, and behaviors, do you feel they have an accurate sense of self?

6. When your child has made a mistake, do they admit it and ask for help (or forgiveness, depending on the circumstance)?

7. Does your child demonstrate a measure of initiative when confronted with a problem?

8. In social settings, do they easily interact with others or do they tend to hang back?

9. Does your child dominate conversations, or do they follow the give-and-take nature of interpersonal interactions?

10. If prompted, do you believe that your child could accurately and thoughtfully describe other people's emotions?

11. If your child has successfully identified the emotions of others, do you believe they would be able to navigate whatever comes with these feelings without your help?

12. How often do you talk to your children about your own emotions and experiences?

13. How often do you ask your children about their emotions and experiences?

14. When you and your child have discussions centered around emotions, do you find that they are able to express themselves clearly while also listening to your responses?

15. Imagine your child sitting in a group of their agemates. Do you believe that your child would willingly strike up a conversation or initiate play with another child if they perceived the latter to be uncomfortable or excluded?

Chapter 2:

Finding the Right Parenting

Style for You

If we don't shape our kids, they will be shaped by outside forces that don't care what shape our kids are in. –Louise Hart

As we enter the second chapter, our understanding of emotional intelligence is firmly in place. We understand its function, its presentation in ourselves and our children, as well as how cultivating a strong EI may be to everyone's benefit. The next step on our road towards setting our children up for success is to determine which route we will take to get there. This choice involves the parenting style we decide to employ when raising our children. Of all the decisions we will make as parents, this is perhaps the most important.

Throughout the course of this chapter, we will explore the different parenting styles we can employ, how their techniques will affect our children, and how we can go about adopting the practices of the styles considered more healthy. Once more, we are exploring ways in which to change our lives. As you move through this chapter, remember that being weary of change is understandable. However, if you ever hope for your child to have a rich emotional life, this change is of the utmost importance and will only serve to make things better for your entire household.

Parenting by the Numbers

There are four different parenting styles, each of which comes with its own set of benefits, disadvantages, characteristics, and techniques. The four parenting styles we will discuss in this chapter are authoritative, authoritarian, permissive, and uninvolved. Right off the bat, we must acknowledge the fact that the authoritative style of parenting is thought by many to be the best of the four. People within the industries of childcare, psychology, and development have identified this style as being the most balanced. Additionally, its benefits are thought to be the most profound as well as the widest-ranging (Li, 2018a).

Popular preference for authoritative parenting aside, these styles have a storied history in the realm of child psychology. Developmental psychologist Diana Baumrind first conceptualized a model involving three distinct approaches to parenting. She argued for the existence of authoritative, authoritarian, and permissive parenting. Moreover, Baumrind posited that there was a close link between the style implemented by parents and the behaviors exhibited by their children (Li, 2018a).

Two decades after Baumrind's theory was created, Eleanor Maccoby and John Martin of Stanford University added the fourth style to the roster. Their 1983 research divided the permissive parenting style into two different styles: The first remained permissive, while the second was an entirely new style known as "neglectful" (Li, 2018). Despite the fact that the theory of parenting styles was conceptualized and worked on first by one person and later by two, no attribution is made in modern times. Some people might talk about Baumrind's parenting styles, while others call them the Maccoby and Martin parenting styles. The name itself doesn't matter; the specifics of each style are what's really important.

Over the course of this chapter, we will go through each of the four parenting styles in detail. However, before we do so, there are some things that are important to note. Firstly, when it comes to the way you parent, we cannot qualitatively distinguish between right and wrong. While certain styles may be more conducive to healthy development than others, raising a child is a complex, nuanced endeavor. Keep this in mind as we move forward. If you discover you are employing parenting techniques that do more harm than good, remind yourself that it is a learning process and that there is no such thing as a perfect parent.

This brings us to the second point of interest: Knowing when to adapt. Parents who are truly successful in their attempts at raising happy, healthy, and well-developed children know that nothing is set in stone. Human beings are inherently capable of change, and if you find that your parenting style isn't yielding the results you hoped for, you can always take a step back, readjust your approach, and try again. This counts not only for your overall method of parenting but also for your actions in the moment. In our day-to-day lives as parents, we are constantly changing tack depending on the situation in which we find ourselves. Some might call for a more authoritarian approach, while others will require you to take a back seat and let your child make their own way. Parenting is an ever-evolving experience, and we must lean into its malleability if we hope to see ourselves and our children succeed.

Finally, we round out this section with a fun little titular tie-in. Of the four parenting styles, authoritative parenting is not only the most highly regarded but also the most commonly employed. In the United States, approximately 46% of parents use this style. By contrast, 10% use the newest style, neglectful; 18% of parents are permissive; and 26% are authoritarians.

Across the country's population, the distribution of parenting styles is relatively stable. However, there is a 2% likelihood that European-American parents will be authoritative, whereas the same percentage of probability is attached to Asian-American parents' use of the authoritarian style (Li, 2018a).

Type 1: The Permissive or Indulgent Parent

Now that we understand what a parenting style is and where it comes from, we can dive straight into the first of the four. Permissive parenting is also called indulgent parenting and is characterized by a high level of responsiveness coupled with a low level of demand on the part of the parent. What this means is that indulgent parents are extremely attentive to their children's emotional needs and respond to these needs regularly and comprehensively. However, this attentiveness comes with a lack of forcefulness in parenting. Permissive parents will have difficulty setting boundaries and limits for their children. When they do put these restrictions in place, their enforcement practices are often nonexistent, and the setting itself may take place irregularly, if at all (Li, 2019a).

The Habits and Regularly-Employed Phrases of a Permissive Parent

As with any other thing that is categorized, permissive parenting has certain habits that characterize this particular style. Parents who are indulgent will routinely avoid implementing overt discipline. In some cases, this means ignoring their child's bad behavior entirely, while in others, it may mean supporting their children as they make their own decisions. Regardless of the context, permissive parents will habitually reject the idea that they must keep their children's behavior under control (Dewar, 2019).

This lack of assertiveness is often coupled with handing the reins over to the children and encouraging the practice of self-regulation. Permissive parents won't make demands on their children, nor will they assign them many responsibilities. In conjunction with this, children of permissive parents will often be encouraged to subvert the standards and expectations of the adults around them, if not reject them entirely. While indulgent parents are encouraging this "make-your-own-way" perspective, they are also often hesitant to assign any authority to themselves. When presenting themselves as parents to their children, they will actively avoid assuming a position of power and may not even encourage their children to look to them as role models or guides. Permissive parents may later subvert their own rejection of power by resorting to things such as manipulation to get their way. This is an extreme example, however, as most permissive parents will end up assuming some sort of authority when attempting to get their way. In instances like these, they will employ logic to reason with their children and will position their own knowledge and experience as superior. This, once again, demonstrates their lack of consistency when it comes to boundaries.

In addition to trademark habits, permissive parents will usually respond to their children in the same way when prompted. Most commonly, an indulgent parent will meet any request or question from their children with the word "yes" (Dewar, 2019). In addition to this, permissive parents may often employ variations of any of the following phrases:

- It isn't my place to tell you what to do.

- You should do what you think is right.

- Even though I'm your parent, I really want you to think of me as your friend.

- Whatever makes you happy.

- You know that I'm not like other parents; you can tell me anything you want.

These phrases may be used in a variety of contexts, though parents will usually employ them in order to avoid any overt displays of power. It should be noted, however, that some phrases that characterize permissive parenting can be used in more positive situations. Sometimes, parents may tell their children these things in order to win their confidence or to let them know that they are supportive of their decisions, dreams, and desires.

Common Traits of a Permissive Parent

Along with the habits and phrases associated with permissive parents, they may also exhibit certain personality and behavioral traits during their attempts at parenting. Li (2019a) describes these traits as follows:

- Parents treat their children with warmth and are extremely emotionally responsive.

- Children are provided with a lot of freedom and are given the autonomy to make decisions on their own.

- Parents will rarely respond with the word "no" when their children ask for something, be it a possession or permission to do something.

- Parents will feel uncomfortable assuming a position of authority within the household. As such, they will not be consistent with their monitoring, guiding, or regulation of their children's behavior.

- Parents will very rarely commit to setting a concrete set of rules for their children. When these rules are set, they will be inconsistently enforced, if not forgotten entirely.

- Given their encouragement of children's rejection of adult expectations and standards, parents will encourage children to make their own decisions. This freedom will be applied to choices large and small, and may even include those meant to fall under the purview of an adult caretaker.

- Very little, if any, guidance will be provided when children are prompted or required to make a decision.

- Children will be given very little responsibility in the house, if any. When tasks such as chores are assigned, the parent is likely not to ensure the child follows through.

In addition to these traits, high responsiveness and low demand also translate into two distinct traits. Interestingly, these traits are somewhat contradictory. The first is described as the capacity for warmth and emotional nurturing, which are beneficial to the child's development. On the other hand, permissive parents also tend to be reluctant to impose any sort of authority and to guide their children, which may prove detrimental down the line (Dewar, 2019). The contrasting nature of these traits presents us with an interesting aspect of this parenting style. Like so many other things in the world of child-rearing, the ins and outs of permissive parenting aren't exactly black and white. While we will explore this style's effect in more depth later on in this chapter, it's worth noting now that many of the traits we find in indulgent parents can be either positive or negative, depending on the context in which they are displayed.

Free-Range Parenting

The nebulous nature of permissive parenting lends itself perfectly to the discussion of our next point: the practice of free-range parenting. Described as a similar-yet-different style when compared to permissive parenting, free-range parenting is described as a technique that enables children to make their own decisions and learn from them, all without parental intervention (Lovering, 2022).

This parenting style is often connected to that of permissive parenting, given the fact that both are characterized by a significant allowance of freedom for the children. In the case of free-range parenting, children are taught the essential skills they need to get by and then allowed certain freedoms based on their age and developmental level. It's worth noting that there is still much to be learned about free-range parenting, as this particular style is less than 20 years old. The first mention of its techniques was introduced to the world in Lenore Skenanzy's 2008 article for the *New York Sun* entitled "Why I Let My 9-Year-Old Ride the Subway Alone" (Morin, 2020). The child-rearing approach described by Skenanzy in this article laid the groundwork for what we know today as free-range parenting.

It is essential that we understand what free-range parenting truly is. For a start, the basic premise of this parenting style is that children should be allowed the necessary freedom to experience the natural consequences of their choices and behaviors. Crucially, this freedom isn't granted from the get-go but rather when the parents determine that the child is ready to handle the responsibility. In doing so, parents hope to teach their children the essential skills they require to grow into responsible, emotionally intelligent adults.

Free-range parenting is a relatively subjective practice. The style's underlying theory presents no guidance as to when children are ready for freedom or how much of it should be doled out. Instead, it's up to the parents themselves to decide when their children have hit enough developmental milestones to be granted this privilege. This brings us to an interesting point regarding free-range parenting. Many conflate the style with that of permissive parenting, largely due to the hands-off techniques that characterize both styles. However, a free-range parent is decidedly not an indulgent one, and their difference is seen in one key trait. Free-range parents are heavily involved in their children's development. They teach their kids skills and check in on how they do with them. Once the parents are satisfied that their children have a firm grasp of these capabilities, only then are they given freedom of commensurate value. Permissive parenting lacks all of the above.

This is not to say that this style of parenting, as unorthodox as it may seem to some, is without its benefits. First and foremost, free-range children encounter the sensation of failure earlier in life than their peers. Through these experiences, they can learn that failing is natural and temporary, and that it is not the set outcome for everything they do. This parenting style is also said to help cultivate problem-solving and critical thinking skills. Moreover, those in favor of this parenting style argue that the lack of parental intervention builds confidence and creativity, and that children's social development also benefits from the techniques of free-range parenting (Lovering, 2022).

Naturally, in the interest of fairness, it must be said that free-range does have a number of drawbacks. The freedoms afforded by these types of parents may increase the probability of children being exposed to serious dangers while away from parental supervision. Moreover, coping with these risks may be beyond the child's skill set, which can have serious, if not disastrous, consequences. Finally, we must consider the very nebulous nature of free-range parenting as one of its greatest disadvantages. (Lovering, 2022). Because parents are the ones who decide when children are ready for more freedom, they may sometimes give children too much free rein and saddle them with more control than they are ready for. This will prove overwhelming for the child soon enough and may cause problems down the road as well.

Associated Outcomes and Effects on Child Development

Returning now to permissive parenting, we must consider that there is a reason why this style has been labeled the worst of the four conceptualized by Baumrind all those years ago. Extensive research has been done into the effects of indulgent parenting on the child, and the following have been identified as the most prevalent:

- Increased impulsiveness.

- Increased aggression.

- A lessened capacity for self-regulation.

- Worse performance in academic environments.

- An increased probability of obesity and other physical health issues.

In terms of child development, permissive parenting is promoted as an approach that sets children up for success more thoroughly than other styles. The idea behind this is that by allowing children to be free and in control of their own lives, they gain life skills quicker and are essentially emotionally better off than other children. Permissive parenting has been shown to yield children with high levels of resourcefulness and self-esteem, as well as children who possess strong problem-solving skills (Dewar, 2019).

On the flip side of this, self-discipline and responsibility tend to be less of an emotional strength for children raised by permissive parents. There's a sort of snowball effect there, as we see the lack of inhibition become extremely detrimental as kids externalize emotional behaviors. This is a fancy way of saying that they feel their emotions strongly and almost always act on them. Finally, we must consider the effect of little to no structure in the home. Dewar (2019) reports that children of indulgent parents very rarely get adequate sleep and that they develop poor sleeping habits. This is because their parents do not help them create a nighttime routine at a young age, something that would play directly into an exhibition of authority.

What to Do if You Are a Permissive Parent

As we know, adopting the mentality of a permissive parent may be helpful from time to time when confronted with some of your children's behaviors. Employing this parenting style full-time, however, can prove to be extremely detrimental. If you have discovered that you are a permissive parent, don't worry too much. Going back to the overall message of this book, you are more than capable of making a positive change in your parenting approach. If it has come to your attention that your parenting practices are overly indulgent, you can remedy the situation by trying the following:

- Set a decisive, audible intention: Realizing you are a permissive parent is one thing; admitting it is quite another. You must take these two steps first in order to begin the process. Next, communicate your intention to change out loud, whether to your spouse, co-parent, or any other member of your support network. Naturally, you must say it to yourself as well. However, verbalizing your intention to others helps make it concrete and will enable you to be held accountable for the actions you take in pursuit of your goal.

- Make your children feel more involved: You don't necessarily need to share your intention with your kids, but making them aware of the changes you'll be making is essential. Talk to them about the new rules and boundaries you will be setting, as well as how they will be enforced. Ensure that this is a healthy, two-way discussion by asking them which changes they feel are necessary and how they feel you can guide them.

- Decide on an approach when it comes to punishments and consequences: Have this discussion with whomever is helping you raise your children, and inform the kids of what you have decided. Remember that your responses must be proportional and must use the principle of natural consequence as opposed to that of out-and-out punishment.

- Follow through: This may be the hardest step of all, but it is definitely the most important. You have to stick to your guns and enforce the new structure you have built in your household. Something that might help you do this is to make sure that your discipline is based on natural consequences. That way, you can teach your children that their actions have repercussions and that it is their responsibility to deal with these aftereffects. Moreover, doing this will allow you to sidestep the mantle of the "bad guy," as you will be educating your children about the way the world works.

Child-rearing is always a team sport when more than one adult is involved. If you hope to have your children reap the benefits of an improved parenting style, you must include your spouse in the process of change. This starts with an open conversation. Talk to your spouse about the realizations you have come to regarding your approach to parenting. Next, tell them of your intention to change the dynamic between you and your children, as well as among all the members of your family. Honesty is essential. You must communicate your needs and desires as they relate to parenting. Tell your spouse what you need from them during the course of this process, whether it be support or a contribution.

However important having this conversation is, it's important that you consider the fact that it might not deliver the result you hope for. Your partner might not be willing to change with you or may wish to stick to their own parenting style, believing it to be successful enough. Though far from ideal, this outcome will force you to follow through on your plans to adopt a different parenting style. In the long run, it will be better for your children to have at least one parent who gives their lives some structure and direction. Who knows? Maybe, at some point down the road, your efforts will inspire your spouse to follow suit.

Type 2: The Uninvolved or Neglectful Parent

Our foray into the world of parenting styles continues. Unfortunately, our exploration isn't trending upward just yet. In the preceding section, we learned that many people view permissive parenting as the worst style of child-rearing. However, whatever degree of negativity people feel about this parenting style is tripled when it comes to an uninvolved parent. This approach to parenting is marked by parents who respond to their children's needs with the bare minimum. Beyond providing them with food, shelter, and clothing, very little caretaking actually happens. Moreover, the level of demand and expectation for their children felt by these parents is exceptionally low (Higuera, 2019b).

Neglectful parenting is the newest of the four styles to be classified and described, and yet it has made quite an impression on parenting groups the world over. Regrettably, this style lives in infamy rather than renown. This is due in large part to the fact that the level of responsiveness demonstrated by these parents is negligible. When we compare it to the responsiveness of permissive parents, who are laissez-faire yet emotionally involved, they appear to be polar opposites. Uninvolved parents basically leave their children to fend for themselves and take charge of their own growth. The children of these parents receive very little, emotionally speaking. Their parents won't provide them with nurturing, discipline, or guidance.

The Habits and Regularly-Employed Phrases of a Neglectful Parent

Each of Baumrind's four parenting styles has its own set of trademark habits. Of the four, these are perhaps the most overt signs of neglectful parenting. That being said, this overtness is limited to those who are involved in the parenting process. Spotting an uninvolved parent from the outside may be difficult, given the fact that they generally do very little in the way of child-rearing. In fact, the habit that characterizes this particular parenting style is the active, continuous rejection of parental obligations (Higuera, 2019b). Along with this, neglectful parents do their best to sidestep any engagement with things related to their children's needs, whether they are expressed as needs, desires, or problems.

It's worth noting that not all neglectful parents utilize this style consciously. Sometimes parents are busy (more on this in a moment) or find other parts of their lives too overwhelming to give their parenting practices the attention they deserve. Crucially, neglectful parents habitually fail to make time to spend with their children and may make no effort to do so at all. Along with avoiding quality time, these parents also tend to gloss over or ignore their children's problems and needs. Instead of attending to what their kids need, these parents will first and foremost deal with their own issues, leaving those of the children to become an afterthought.

Naturally, this afterthought is accompanied by a lack of interest in just about everything their children do. Neglectful parents fail to muster any sort of emotional investment in their children's activities, performance at school, or indeed any other part of their lives. These parents will habitually refrain from attending important meetings, significant events, or anything that requires them to play the role of a parent for the duration of the experience.

However, because neglectful parents don't always employ this style knowingly, they may use certain phrases to explain away their behavior. It must be noted that parents who are deliberately and consciously uninvolved may also use these phrases if only to make their neglect appear less overt. Parents who employ this style of child-rearing will often say any of the following:

- I don't have the time to do that.

- You're old enough to handle that on your own.

- That doesn't really sound like my sort of thing, but you can tell me all about it later.

- Do whatever you want.

- Figure it out on your own.

- The only way you'll learn is by doing it yourself.

Common Traits of a Neglectful Parent

The habits of a neglectful parent do not simply spring into existence. They are, in fact, informed by many of the different traits that parents who employ this style display. According to Li (2020), uninvolved parenting is characterized by the following traits:

- Demonstration of little to no emotional warmth or affection on the part of the parent.

- Feeling no need to connect with the children or cultivate a healthy attachment style, if any at all.

- Feeling no compulsion, obligation, or desire to provide emotional support for their children, both in times of distress and in times of stability.

- Perpetuating a cycle of neglect and little involvement that started during their own childhood.

- Feel no sense of expectation for their children with regards to achievement.

- Inability to spend quality time with their children.

- Putting off or avoiding parental responsibilities.

You will notice that some of these traits may be seen as direct causes of avoidant parental behavior. Others may be used unconsciously when parents are too busy or preoccupied (more on this in a moment) and may lead to inadvertent neglect. Additionally, you may notice that some of these traits are inherited from the parenting style utilized by an uninvolved parent's own caregivers. While we cannot excuse the harm that negligence causes if it is inherited, understanding the effect of your childhood on your own parenting practices is extremely important. This is true for each of the parenting styles we discuss in this chapter.

Busy Versus Uninvolved

You will have noticed that, through our exploration of this particular parenting style, we have made mention of the fact that uninvolved parenting may be done unintentionally. In order to explore this more fully, we must examine what it means to be a neglectful parent as opposed to a parent who is simply busy.

Parents who fall into the latter category are those who find themselves taken away from parenting time and activities by the demands of something such as their work. Like their uninvolved counterparts, busy parents don't have much time to engage with or spend with their children. However, there is a key difference between these two types of parents, and it all comes down to interest and involvement. Despite the fact that their schedules may be packed to the brim, busy parents are still interested in what's going on in their children's lives. Moreover, they are emotionally invested in their well-being, display warmth towards them, and will nurture them as best they can (Li, 2020).

It is essential that we differentiate between the two, as a busy parent's lack of availability does not always equate to neglect. It is also important that we understand that the impact of a parent's efforts and the emotional relationship that results from them aren't contingent on the number of hours they log in proximity to their children. On the surface, a busy parent may appear uninvolved. What differentiates them from those parents who truly don't care is the fact that they will try to make up for lost time. In instances like these, we must understand that quality parent-child time is more impactful than being around your child for extended periods of time and doing very little to foster a bond with them. At the end of the day, it all comes down to effort.

Associated Outcomes and Effects on Child Development

As we've already established, uninvolved parenting is unilaterally regarded as the worst of the parenting styles described by Diana Baumrind. The placement of this style at the very bottom of the ranking is due in large part to the effects it has on children. The majority of these effects have been described as negative and have been identified as follows:

- Increased impulsiveness.

- Decreased levels of self-control and inhibition.

- Poor social skills.

- Decreased ability to self-regulate emotions.

- Increased risk for the development of serious mental health issues.

- Increased risk for the development of substance use disorder. This particular effect is much more prevalent in children who were raised by uninvolved parents who were dealing with addiction themselves (Li, 2020).

- Lower levels of overall academic achievement.

Though most of the consequences of neglectful parenting have been classified as detrimental, there are some effects that have slightly positive connotations. Children who are raised using this parenting style have demonstrated elevated levels of independence and a strong sense of self-reliance. These children are able to identify their needs as well as the actions they need to take in order to fulfill them. Regrettably, this is where the positives begin and end. In the case of this parenting style, the negatives far outweigh the positives, as children from neglectful homes may find their emotional development stunted or delayed. Later in life, this may lead them to engage in relationships that are unhealthy or abusive. Conversely, they may also demonstrate high levels of emotional need or codependence as compensation for the lack of warmth and connection they experienced during childhood.

Type 3: The Authoritarian Parent

Our next stop along the tour of parenting styles takes us to the other end of the spectrum of parent-child engagement. The authoritarian parenting style has gained quite a bit of notoriety, largely due to its structure, which Dewar (2018) describes as "little nurturing, lots of psychological control."

The third of the four parenting styles are characterized by a drastically uneven distribution between the parents' expectations of their children and their responsiveness. It is important to remember when we talk about parenting styles and their levels of expectation and response that these parts of a parent-child relationship are largely transactional. If parents set incredibly high standards for their children and expect them to achieve a great deal of impressive feats, the rules of emotional intelligence would dictate that children receive support, warmth, and nurturing in return for their efforts. With authoritarian parents, regrettably, the emotional power that is meant to be distributed equally flows very much in one direction only.

Before we explore this parenting style in more detail, it's worth referring back to the concept of parenting as a heritable trait. Very often, when people become parents for the first time, they seek to emulate the practices and techniques employed by their own parents. You may have done this yourself. That's fine; in fact, it's perfectly natural. Your childhood is your first and best frame of reference for what parenting involves. As such, you will find that many authoritarian parents come from households with a similar parent-child dynamic. While we can't lay all the blame for who we are at our parents' feet, looking back on your childhood may prove beneficial to your parenting journey. Even if you don't learn anything, the insight alone is worthwhile.

The Habits and Regularly-Employed Phrases of an Authoritarian Parent

In terms of behavioral habits, our look at authoritarian parenting takes us into a realm of emotional intensity. The first thing we encounter is the setting of intensely strict rules and boundaries. Not only will these be maintained and enforced, but they may often be used as a gauge of weakness or insubordination. Many authoritarian parents are of the belief that when their children cross a boundary or break a rule, they are flagrantly disrespecting the parents' efforts. We see this happen, whether the indiscretion was conscious or not. This leads us to the second habit of authoritarian parents, which is to respond to moments of emotional distress or divergence with raised voices and aggression (Li, 2019b).

One of the most famous habits of authoritarian parents is that they micromanage just about every aspect of their children's lives. Some parents who employ this style will go so far as to dictate the precise manner in which their children ought to dress, walk, talk, and even think. It may not come as a surprise, but authoritarian parents aren't all that open to feedback. As such, they regularly employ the following phrases:

- Don't question me!

- You will do so because I am your parent, and I have given you an instruction.

- If you question or doubt me, you are disrespecting me as a parent and undermining my authority.

- You will do exactly as I tell you, or there will be severe consequences.

- Not only have you disrespected me, but you have also let me down immensely.

Many times, the phrases employed by an authoritarian parent are intended as a means of keeping their children obedient, but they may sometimes cross over into manipulation. Furthermore, it's worth noting that, in the most extreme of cases, this parenting style has the potential to become abusive, whether physically, emotionally, verbally, or otherwise.

Common Traits of an Authoritarian Parent

Li (2019b) describes the attributes of an authoritarian parent along the lines of coldness and distance. Dewar (2018) outlines the traits of these parents in a similar way and emphasizes the role that control plays in parent-child relationships forged in authoritarian households. From these sources, we understand the traits of an authoritarian parent as follows:

- Communication takes place, but only from the parent to the child. Feedback of any kind regarding parenting techniques, rules, schedules, or the like is strongly discouraged or ignored.

- A lot of emphasis is placed on status and prestige, and standards are set incredibly high in order to maintain the family's reputation.

- Control is of the essence for the parent, and they may exert it through shaming, yelling, purposefully limiting their warmth and love, and handing down strict and unyielding punishments.

- Rarely, if ever, do they motivate their parenting decisions and regard themselves as the highest authority in the household. This sense of authority is often thought to be infallible.

- Believe that warmth and profound emotional connection are earned through achievements and acquiescence.

- Very little consideration is given to the emotional state, desires, or wishes of the children. Instead, the parent's goals for their children are prioritized.

- Some authoritarian parents may live vicariously through their children and pursue the life they never had.

When we list the traits of an authoritarian parent, it does appear as though they don't have their child's best interests at heart. Naturally, parental motivations will vary from person to person. However, the fact that authoritarian parents are so heavily involved in their children's lives is somewhat indicative of their wish for success and happiness for their kids. True, their methods may be unorthodox and somewhat severe, but these parents are invested in their children's development and will do all they can to set them up for success. Unfortunately, this goal may be set for better or worse.

Advantages and Disadvantages of The Authoritarian Parenting Style

I'm going to level with you; so far, things don't look all that good for the authoritarian parenting style. However, if there is one thing we have learned thus far, it is that nothing in the realm of parenting is ever entirely black or white. This parenting style is somewhat mixed. Though we will explore its outcomes and effects in the following section, we can already identify some of the advantages and disadvantages of the authoritarian style. In fact, we can condense each of the style's positive and negative points into two distinct aspects: connection and performance.

The first, unfortunately, is the greatest disadvantage of authoritarian parenting. As much as children gain in skills and competence, they lose in the strength of the bond they hold with their parents. When we consider how authoritarian parents treat and use the concepts of warmth and affection, it should come as no surprise that they tend not to form close attachment bonds with their children. This is especially true when nurturing is used as a bargaining chip to motivate children to attain certain achievements.

In parent-child relationships where displays of love are contingent on performance or obedience, we may see the development of unhealthy attachment bonds as well as those that are weak. Children may become codependent during adulthood, as authoritarian parenting can result in difficulties when it comes to emotional intelligence (Li, 2019b).

On the flip side, we can look at performance as one of the aspects of life that authoritarian parenting tends to improve. When children are pushed to maintain a high standard of work in each of their pursuits, they may enjoy the fruits of their labors in the form of success. It should be noted, however, that this is not guaranteed, as motivation-based performance is a tricky thing to navigate. When the motivation is internal (see the markers of high EI), success is more easily achieved. However, if it is external and that motivator is removed or softened, people may find that they have a hard time following through. All-in-all, we may have to come to terms with the fact that the harshness of authoritarian parenting means that the scales of outcome are tipped heavily towards the side of disadvantage.

Associated Outcomes and Effects on Child Development

By now, we have a relatively solid idea of what constitutes authoritarian parenting. If we consider all we have learned and cast our minds back to the section covering neglectful parenting, we may find that the designation of the worst style is up for debate. Regardless of which parenting style may, in fact, be the most damaging, it's safe to say that authoritarian parents tend to do more harm than good. Many of the effects of this parenting style relate to emotional development and intelligence. Children from authoritarian homes may encounter severe difficulty as they move through the process of emotional maturation. In addition to this, authoritarian parenting has been shown to affect children in the following ways:

- Increased and more intense experiences of unhappiness, especially if they are unable to achieve goals. This is true for goals set by the child as well as those set by their parents.

- Decreased levels of independence.

- Tendencies toward impulsivity and poor emotional regulation.

- Intense, maladaptive, externalized emotional behaviors when away from their home environment.

- Poor social skills.

- Lower self-esteem and resilience.

- Increased vulnerability to the development of psychological disorders such as obsessive-compulsive disorder (OCD) and post-traumatic stress disorder (PTSD).

Does Tough Love Work?

Oftentimes, authoritarian parents will justify their strictness and lack of flexibility by claiming that they are simply practicing "tough love" (Li, 2019b). Many parents will label their style this way or say that they are relying on more traditional, old-school methods. In truth, though the name may differ, tough love parenting is simply authoritarian parenting with a slightly snappier name. If there is any difference to speak of, it is simply that the former is regarded as a subtype of the latter.

Tough love is the go-to style for many parents, particularly those who grew up in authoritarian homes themselves. However, despite the slight difference in name, tough love is largely the same as authoritarian parenting. Tough love is motivated by the idea that harshness and the restriction of parental warmth will strengthen a child emotionally. Moreover, parents using these methods believe that they are teaching their children to be disciplined, to appreciate the value of authority, to adopt positive, constructive behaviors, and to set them up for success.

Unfortunately, this rigidity and the emotional distance it creates between parents and their children largely yield the same results as any other form of authoritarian parenting. In fact, if we consider the fact that many parents use their own childhoods as references when parenting for the first time, there is a distinct possibility that tough love parenting pushes children to become more emotionally open, generous, and vulnerable later in life. The opposite may also be true, and this parenting style may breed children who are emotionally closed off and hold the same rigid views of the world as their parents.

Tiger Parenting

We conclude our exploration of authoritarian parenting by examining a second, perhaps equally famous, form of the style. First described by Amy Chua in her 2011 book *Battle Hymn of the Tiger Mom*, tiger parenting is described as an extremely strict, authority-based method of parenting intended to cultivate high achievers (Plant, 2021).

This parenting style is based on principles similar to those of tough love, with parents employing its techniques because they feel it will teach their children strong work ethics, and they do so by setting incredibly high standards. Ideally speaking, these tactics will prove effective, and children will learn the value of perseverance, commitment, motivation, and self-discipline. Tiger parents teach their kids to work hard from the get-go so that they may become accustomed to working for what they want.

While tiger parenting does resemble tough love parenting in many ways, the key difference between the two is that this version of the authoritarian style is slightly more malleable. In recent years, tiger parenting has evolved to become less cold and to include more aspects of positive parenting (Plant, 2021). This way, children are still set up for success but are also able to form closer attachment bonds with their parents. That being said, the greatest risk this parenting style poses is tied to children's mental health.

Given the rigidity and harshness that often accompany the methods of tiger parents, children may grow up with an extreme fear of failure. This stems from their fear of punishment when they are unable to meet their parents' standards. This worry translates into adulthood and makes learning through failure all the more difficult. Additionally, tiger parenting may influence children to view traditional achievements as the pinnacle of success. This is the opposite of what we hope to do when raising emotionally intelligent children, as the children of tiger parents will view success in academic and professional settings as the most important achievement of all.

Type 4: The Authoritative Parent

The fourth and final parenting style conceptualized by Baumrind is widely regarded as the best approach to take when it comes to child-rearing. Authoritative parenting is thought to balance the best aspects of parent-child bonding with the most effective strategies that foster an environment of structure and positive discipline. Parents who employ this approach set high standards for their children and expect much of them in the way of achievements. What sets it apart from the other three styles is that authoritative parents match their expectations with their responsiveness. This give-and-take is found throughout all interactions of this parenting style, as parents construct their household to be more-or-less democratic. Children's opinions, preferences, limits, and abilities are recognized and respected. Both within child psychology circles as well as in the minds of the general parenting populace, authoritative parenting is thought to have the best influence on children and contribute the most to their emotional intelligence (Dewar, 2017).

Authoritative Versus Authoritarian

Though the two might sound similar enough (I often mix them up myself), we can't identify too many parallels between authoritative and authoritarian parenting. In fact, the only characteristic present in both parenting styles is the level of demandingness exhibited by parents. In either style, the parents set high standards for their children and aim for them to achieve great feats of success. Unfortunately, this is where the resemblance stops.

When we compare the differences between the two, we see that they diverge the most in the field of parent-child interaction. Authoritarian parents tend to exhibit little-to-no warmth, opting instead to craft a relationship with their child through the assertion of power. They remind kids of their authority as parents, reinforcing the rules and boundaries they have decided to implement. By contrast, authoritative parents tend to avoid explicit declarations of power as well as the setting of hard-line limits without flexibility. Instead, they reinforce the household rules through positive, meaningful emotional interactions. Additionally, they help maintain their authority by explaining the rules to their kids as well as the reasons for their implementation.

Authoritative parents understand that, in order to have their children follow their instructions, they must offer something in return. As such, these parents make sure to take care of their child's emotional needs. They encourage their children to adopt emotionally intelligent behaviors but allow them to do so through self-exploration and by carving their own paths. Authoritarian parents sit at the opposite end of the spectrum, deciding beforehand the behaviors and traits they want their kids to exhibit and pushing them towards acquiescence.

It must be said that both of these parenting styles deliver results, and both have been known to yield high-achieving children. Only one of these styles, however, is able to acquire these results without having to sacrifice the health and strength of the bond they have with their children.

The Habits and Regularly-Employed Phrases of an Authoritative Parent

On the whole, authoritative parents tend to form more emotionally healthy parenting habits. For a start, these parents enforce discipline instead of handing down punishments, and even in the case of the former, they have a gentler touch, explaining the logic behind their rules. Rules are of the essence to authoritative parents, but they will also clue their children in as to what the exact parameters of these rules are as well as what the consequences are for breaking them. This parenting style is marked by transparency and clear communication. Moreover, authoritative parents will make a habit of supporting their children and nurturing their development through positive practices. They will praise their children's efforts and provide them with comfort when they falter. Authoritative parents also tend to engage in fun with their kids so that they may establish a stronger, deeper child-parent bond (Li, 2018b).

When practicing authoritative parenting, the following phrases crop up frequently:

- I know that you are busy this morning, but would you be willing to help me out later?

- How do you feel about what happened at the dinner table tonight? Do you understand why we responded the way we did?

- I'd like to get your opinion on this, and please be honest with me.

- You seem upset today; is everything okay?

- What can I do to help?

- The reason we set these rules is…

- I'm not angry with you; I'm just a little hurt. I would really like it if we could discuss what happened today.

- You gave it your all, and I'm so proud of you for trying!

Common Traits of an Authoritative Parent

As with the three preceding parenting styles, there are certain characteristics that tend to be found in those parents who employ the authoritative style. These traits are as follows:

- Recognize their children's autonomy and factor their unique personhood into parenting decisions.

- Make an effort to be tuned into their child's emotional needs and desires and do what they can to fulfill them.

- Authoritative parents will be affectionate towards their children and nurture them in the way that will be most conducive to their development.

- Encourage independence so that children can explore the world around them as well as the one that exists within themselves.

- They are consistent in their parenting, upholding rules, limits, and boundaries.

- Will work towards earning their child's respect as opposed to demanding it outright.

- Will encourage their children to share their thoughts and feelings, and will be receptive to this communication.

Associated Outcomes and Effects on Child Development

As we know, authoritative parenting is thought to yield the best results with regards to the child's emotional, cognitive, and social development. These parents allow and encourage their children to individuate, but they also provide them with a safe, structured environment in which to do so. Authoritative parenting effectively walks the line between affording children independence and keeping them committed to rules and boundaries. When we look at the effects that this parenting style has in the long run, we tend to see nothing but positives. Children of authoritative parents have demonstrated:

- Increased happiness, both with their decisions as well as the general state of their lives.

- Increased levels of independence and the easy development of skills tied to self-reliance.

- The tendency to adopt a more positive outlook on life. These children also pay it forward in terms of the warmth and nurturing they received from their parents.

In doing so, they cultivate strong, loving interpersonal relationships.

- Elevated levels of competence in social settings.

- Greater proficiency in practices tied to EI, such as self-control and self-regulation.

- Enhance academic performance, which translates to a stronger work ethic and higher levels of achievement in the workplace.

- The development of strong self-esteem as well as robust self-awareness.

- An overall improved state of mind, experiencing struggles with mental health more infrequently during their lives.

Authoritative Parenting Strategies

In addition to those practices outlined above, we can identify a few other key strategies employed by authoritative parents. First and foremost, we observe the use of inductive discipline, which upholds household rules while simultaneously tasking children with thinking critically. This practice asks kids to think in a constructive manner, with an eye on determining how their behavior affects not only them but also the other members of their household (Dewar, 2017). This strategy aims to have children motivate the exhibition of positive behavior from within as you provide them with the tools of emotional regulation, comprehension, and management to do just that.

Additionally, we see authoritative parents elicit positive behaviors from their children through the use of empathy. We have already encountered empathy and will revisit it later as well, so we have a basic understanding of the practice. In this particular context, empathy is used to construct and supplement a child's intrinsic motivation, which enables them to behave thoughtfully and considerately of their own accord. By helping their children understand the impact of their behaviors, authoritative parents imbue them with moral reasoning skills, which they can then use to determine whether certain actions are appropriate in certain contexts.

These moral reasoning skills are taught in tandem with good old-fashioned logical reasoning. Authoritative parents are transparent about the decisions they make regarding boundaries, rules, and discipline. Crucially, these parents also understand that the development of logical reasoning will need to resonate with their children. In the early years, this means giving explicit instructions and detailing the consequences of deviating from them. Once their children have reached an age at which they can understand more complex concepts, this communication expands to a conversation, and parents share their own reasoning process behind their decisions as well as the different factors that influence their parenting choices.

Finally, authoritative parents help their children enrich and control their emotional state through a hands-on approach, namely emotion coaching. Just like empathy, we will take a more in-depth look at this practice in a later chapter. For now, what we need to know is that emotion coaching means enabling children to understand and label their feelings. Subsequently, the practice fosters a child's ability to construct a solution to the issue at hand and to see its execution through. All of this is done with the support and assistance of an authoritative parent.

Other "Unofficial" Parenting Styles

Baumrind's concept of parenting styles has been around for some time now. However, in recent decades, two more distinct approaches have been added to the list. While these styles aren't officially recognized as part of Baumrind's model, they are employed often enough to warrant discussion.

Helicopter Parenting

This parenting style is characterized by over-involvement. First conceptualized in the 1969 book *Between Parent and Teenager* by Dr. Haim Ginott, helicopter parenting is practiced by parents who are too heavily involved in their children's lives, often to the detriment of the kids. These parents believe that they and they alone must take ownership of their children's experiences, in particular their successes and failures. This parenting style is also sometimes referred to as "cosseting parenting," "bulldoze parenting," or "lawnmower parenting" (Bayless, 2022).

Helicopter parents tend to insert themselves into every single aspect of their children's lives. However, while we can make this observation objectively on paper, in practice, this style is often conflated with that of a simple, engaged parent. In order to identify helicopter parenting, look out for the following signs:

- Allowing their children's interests, activities, desires, and goals to consume them so much that these aspects of their own personhood fall by the wayside.

- Enabling their continued, excessive involvement by actively disregarding their own goals, ambitions, and well-being to one side in order to focus exclusively on their child.

- Placing excessive pressure on children to excel, as they feel these achievements are just as much their own.

- Conversely, parents should actively shield their kids from certain experiences or topics that may be difficult or uncomfortable, as they will assume the impact of these experiences for themselves.

- Attempting to micromanage their children's social lives.

- Scheduling an activity for every minute of every day and believing that this will give their kids an edge over their peers, even where no competition exists.

- Taking pride in this excessive level of involvement and rationalizing it as an expression of love while ensuring their children's needs are met.

These signs may not make helicopter parenting sound all that appealing, but it is not without its positives. Generally speaking, children raised by these parents can be counted on to engage in prosocial behaviors. They are also more likely to receive support and guidance throughout their childhood, which may help them make better decisions. Given the fact that this parenting style is contingent on parents being involved in their kids' lives, we see benefits such as providing their children with environments in which they can feel loved and accepted. Moreover, constant encouragement from parents may lead to greater self-confidence as well as increased self-exploration (Bayless, 2022).

However, if we use words like "overly" and "excessive" to describe this parenting style, we must consider that there are some drawbacks to being a helicopter parent. First and foremost, it can damage the parent-child relationship. If parents constantly step in and manage things on behalf of their kids, children may develop feelings of resentment, as they will believe their parents don't trust them to do things on their own. Additionally, this damage may worsen when children enter adulthood, and their parents aren't there to guide their every action. Because they were never able to adequately develop essential life and coping skills, children of helicopter parents will encounter significant difficulties when faced with obstacles or adversity later in life.

In addition to this, by preventing their kids from taking control, helicopter parents hinder the development of self-advocacy. As a result, their children will be unable to speak and stand up for themselves in moments of difficulty. The constant vigilance of this style may also lead to low self-esteem, as children will feel as though they can do nothing without their parents' input or guidance. Finally, this parenting style effectively sets children up for an adulthood experienced from a warped perspective. Because parents will always step in to shield their children from negative experiences, they will never know how to deal with the natural consequences of their actions, whether good or bad. When they enter adulthood, this may lead to some shock as they start to function in the real world (Phillips, 2019).

If you have some concerns that you are a helicopter parent and would like to change your approach, there are a number of things you can do. Shifting away from helicopter parenting involves:

- Encouraging independence and allowing them to exercise their autonomy.

- Allowing them to see things through on their own and to deal with difficulties or failures.

- Teach and encourage them to express their needs, especially if they need something different from you in terms of emotional support.

- Give them responsibility and ensure that they see these tasks through. You can help if it is absolutely necessary, but they ought to complete these tasks largely by themselves.

- Make an effort to take care of yourself and to pursue your own dreams while helping your child along the path to achieving theirs.

Gentle Parenting

In practice, gentle parenting centers around the strength of the parent-child bond. Introduced to the world in the 1920s by Dr. Alfred Adler, this parenting style is characterized by interactions that are focused on the child's emotional development and well-being. Gentle parenting practices include the facilitation and encouragement of skills such as emotional expression, as well as independence. The attributes are gained in a domestic environment built on love, safety, and comfort. Gentle parents are involved but allow their kids the freedom and space they need to explore (BetterHelp Editorial Team, 2023).

Because of gentle parenting's peaceful approach, one of the most prominent benefits of this style is that it eliminates tension in families and helps prevent resentment from arising between the child and their parent. This relative emotional calm stems from the combination of freedom and limitation this parenting practice employs. While children are encouraged and supported as they explore their world to discover who they are, this exploration isn't limitless. Gentle parents will set boundaries and enforce rules to ensure that their child's journey of self-discovery and expression takes place safely.

In the context of EI, we also see the benefits of gentle parenting on children's social skills. This style has been shown to lead to decreased occurrences of anxiety in children and, as such, enables children to build their self-confidence, assertiveness, and self-advocacy. When they are then presented with new and potentially challenging social situations, the children of gentle parents don't panic but instead navigate these unfamiliar waters with ease and self-assurance. Additionally, this style has been linked to improved academic performance, which is facilitated by a child's self-awareness and knowing what works for them when learning.

However, nothing is perfect, and gentle parenting has been known to elicit concerns of excessive leniency bordering on permissive parenting. Moreover, detractors have pointed out that many of the style's techniques and methods are generic or overly clinical. When this translates to the real world, it results in children having stilted, unnatural conversational skills, which may in fact prove harmful to their socialization abilities.

Given that this parenting style does involve loosening the rules somewhat, both children and parents alike may struggle to cope well with this more relaxed structure. Finally, critics of the parenting style have pointed to the focus on exploration and freedom as being enabling. Parents may allow maladaptive or negative behaviors if they can justify their presence in the name of their child's self-exploration and growth. If this is just a bump in the road, the situation should straighten itself out soon enough, and no further issues will arise from these behaviors. However, if they are sustained, parents risk teaching their children that these actions are acceptable.

Despite the less-than-perfect nature of this style, it is still worth considering implementing some of its practices into your current parenting approach. If you'd like to get started with gentle parenting, you can do the following:

- Start small by simply addressing bad behavior. Do not make this a comment on your child's character. Simply focus on why the action itself was undesirable.

- Model the positive behavior you would like your child to adopt for their emotional development.

- When interacting with your child, remember to be compassionate and kind, and to practice empathy as much as possible.

- Make actions collaborative and lessen their resemblance to instructions.

- Be patient, and help your child.

- Adjust your expectations. Your child is a real human being and will most likely not live up to the image of the ideal you have in your mind. Understand and embrace their humanity.

Positive Discipline Versus Punishment

When addressing bad behavior, it is essential to understand the difference between punishing your child and enforcing positive discipline. We often believe the two to be quite similar, but in practice as well as long-term efficacy, they couldn't be more different.

Punishment

When you punish your child, you are exerting parental control through fear. You introduce a consequence, either physical, emotional, or punitive, and teach your child to fear this consequence if you observe this behavior in them again. Essentially, you are imposing some sort of penalty for behavioral mistakes or missteps (Silm, 2013).

Though punishment may succeed in the moment, this practice isn't very effective, all things considered. This is because you aren't actually teaching your child how to amend or manage their behavior. Instead, you teach them that they will only face consequences if caught but will face no repercussions if you don't find out. Resultantly, they continue these behaviors in secret, and your child learns nothing in the vein of self-control or positive behavioral decision-making. In fact, all that punishment does is lead your child toward rebellion and actions that will keep them out of your sight.

Punishment is only effective in the short-term and contributes nothing to your child's emotional development. This is because your child does not learn how to amend their behavior to something more positive, but rather that they need only fear your awareness of the issue. In the process, no skills linked to EI are gained, and the parent-child bond may start to weaken.

Discipline

Positive discipline is goal-oriented and focuses on teaching your child self-control and emotional regulation so that they can make informed, positive behavioral decisions (Silm, 2013). This practice takes a more holistic approach by teaching your child about the bigger picture, in which they can see how their behavior affects others. Additionally, they are also able to understand that the consequences of their actions are entirely due to their behavioral choices. While this teaches them accountability, it also helps them understand that they have control over what they do, which in turn may lead to better decision-making in the future.

Discipline is nearly the polar opposite of punishment, as it engages in techniques that will pay off in the long term by helping your child learn emotional regulation, impulse control, and which behaviors are appropriate when. When you implement positive discipline, you don't assume that your child's actions were motivated by any sort of malicious intent but that they resulted from human error and not knowing better. These behavioral missteps are treated as learning opportunities and are used to teach children new emotional skills. Most important of all, discipline is proactive and uses a mistake in the present to help avoid a potentially worse repetition down the line.

Navigating Parenting Styles

With all the different parenting styles that exist, both official and off-the-books, it can be difficult to know which one will work best for you. This decision is further complicated when you consider that no one approach is entirely perfect. If you are experiencing difficulty determining whether to become authoritative, permissive, gentle, or even indulgent, consider the following:

- As we know, authoritative parenting is widely regarded as the best parenting style. Though we have already enumerated its many benefits, keep in mind that this approach is known to yield children who are socially competent, independent, self-reliant, and overall well-adjusted.

- When it comes to parenting, there is no such thing as "one size fits all." The particulars of any given parenting style can be heavily influenced by factors such as culture, religion, and socioeconomic status. As such, the same style may look different across the world. It is also important to remember that people don't exist in black and white. You don't have to commit to a single parenting style for as long as you live. Different situations will call for different approaches and solutions. Sometimes you will have to be slightly authoritarian, while other times, you may have to become more permissive and learn to let go. However, you must remember to do this in moderation, as swinging between styles too often can prove just as detrimental as sticking to only one with unmoving rigidity.

- Consider who your child is when selecting a style. Take their temperament, disposition, and personality into account. If your child requires more structure and guidance, look for styles that include firm rules and boundaries. If you fear your child is too sheltered or set in their ways, consider the styles that will allow them a bit more freedom to make mistakes, get some life experience, and discover new things about themselves.

- Remember that scientific data cannot always accurately portray the reality of parenting. Famously, we know that correlation does not equal causation. Just because certain results have been observed under certain parenting styles does not mean that you can only achieve similar goals by changing your parenting approach. Consider the context in which you are parenting, and remember that real life is more complicated than clinical studies describe.

What to Do When You Can't Agree With Your Partner on a Parenting Style

Parenting is difficult enough in and of itself. However, if we add into the mix the possibility that two parents may approach child-rearing in completely different ways, things become significantly more complex. If you find that you and your partner are in disagreement regarding the style that is best suited to your household and your children, you need to find a way of dealing with this before the divergence causes lasting damage.

First and foremost, figure out what your parenting style is and why you chose it. By understanding why you parent the way you do, you can explain to your partner why you prefer your approach. You can also share with them what you hope to accomplish through its use. Afford them the opportunity to do the same with their parenting style, and see if there is some middle ground you can access to employ the best aspects of either approach.

If your practical implementation of your style differs vastly, consider setting up rules for your children based on shared values. Agree on what these rules are as well as what the consequences will be for any infractions. While you and your partner may not execute discipline in the same way, your children will still understand why they are being reprimanded and won't be confused about the consequences of their actions.

Perhaps most important of all is the support you have for one another. Despite the fact that parenting isn't an "us versus them" endeavor, your children may seek to exploit any discord they notice when observing your parenting styles. As such, present a united front in front of your children, especially when it comes to discipline. If you disagree with your partner's decisions or actions, wait until you are alone to unpack the issue and come up with a solution for the next time you encounter a similar situation. Additionally, don't let your differences cloud your judgment. Your parenting style may make certain things easier for you than for your partner. If you see them struggling, step in and help them. You can devise a signal or code word you can use to communicate a need for assistance.

Finally, remember to take care of your relationship with your children. You and your partner will be able to overcome differences and difficulties more easily if your bond is healthy and you are happy in the relationship. Make time to spend with one another to remain close and to be reminded of your love for one another. You can use this time to talk through some of your issues, both parental and otherwise. Maintaining a healthy relationship will make cooperation easier and will go a long way towards creating a peaceful household environment.

Positive Parenting Tips

Positive parenting is an approach that lies outside of any particular parenting style and focuses on teaching kids behavioral control while facilitating positive, healthy development. This practice involves teaching through kindness, nurturing, and warmth with the ultimate aim of guiding our children towards behaviors that will contribute positively to their lives (University of California, Davis Health, 2023). Adopting positive parenting techniques needn't be difficult. You can set your child up for healthy development through the following methods:

- Be consistent: By providing your child with routines and structure, you teach them how to follow through and the importance of doing the things others expect of you. Having a regular routine helps them understand which behaviors are suited to which contexts and gives them a framework from which to make their own behavioral decisions.

- Praise their efforts, but try to avoid giving rewards: Though your child can most certainly do with your support and encouragement, don't let this go beyond words or actions of praise and affirmation. If you reward your child, you teach them to embrace a "tit-for-tat" mentality. If this continues long enough, they may become entitled, expecting some sort of reward for performing the actions tied to their responsibilities. Avoiding rewards may also help them develop intrinsic motivation.

- Make use of disciplinary tactics as opposed to punishment: This is fairly self-explanatory, as we have already covered the importance of discipline over punitive action. Embrace positive parenting by using misbehavior as a teachable moment to set them back on course for more positive behavior.

- Set clear, easy-to-understand household rules: Rules and limits will let you know which behaviors are appropriate and which will lead to disciplinary action. Discuss these rules with them, explaining why you have put them in place and what the consequences will be if they are broken. Though rule-setting can feel overly harsh, it provides your child with much-needed guidance and structure.

- Don't entertain explosive emotions: More often than not, reactivity and tantrums are employed as a mechanism for manipulation. Let your child know that you will not give in by remaining calm and giving them firm instructions to end this behavior. Stick to your guns, and praise them for putting a stop to their misbehavior.

- Take care of your own emotional needs: Remember that you will be modeling behavior for your child. If they see you neglecting your emotional well-being, they may be moved to do the same. Also, being a peaceful parent will become just about impossible if you are stressed, frustrated, or overwhelmed. Make time to engage in some self-care and tend to your emotional needs. Don't forget to lean on your support network for help when you need it.

With that, we have finished laying the theoretical foundation for parenting with a focus on developing emotional intelligence. Now that you understand who you are as a parent and what your approach entails exactly, we can start to become more practical-minded. However, as we move into this next section, remember that Rome wasn't built in a day, and neither will your child's emotional skills be perfected overnight. Begin small and work your way up to handling the biggest of experiences that come with the emotional experience that is human life.

Chapter 3:

Baby Steps

Kids don't do what you say. They do what they see. How you live your life is their example. –Tim Ferriss

Much of our time has been spent examining the theory behind parenthood and its practices. While this information is essential to have, I think it's safe to say that we have the foundational aspects of child-rearing covered by now. We know what type of parent we are, what EI looks like in ourselves and in our children, and how we can adjust our approach to become a more positive parent. With this knowledge now safely filed away in our minds, we can begin to take actionable steps towards raising emotionally intelligent children. In this chapter, we will explore the concept of emotional literacy, how it relates to EI, and how we can go about enabling our children to reap its benefits.

How Soon Can You Begin Teaching Emotional Literacy?

Before we can begin to examine the teaching of emotional literacy at different ages, we must first look at what this concept actually is. In its simplest form, emotional literacy is a term used interchangeably with emotional intelligence. However, despite their near-identical nature, there are some key distinctions to be made between the two. Emotional literacy is a skill that enables a person to identify the reality of their emotional state. In addition to this identification, an emotionally literate person will be able to communicate what they are feeling and express these emotions thoroughly and healthily (Mills, 2016). While this sounds just like the concept of EI, it's important to note that the former is a component of the latter. This awareness and expression are very important, but they form only one part of being an emotionally intelligent person.

Given the importance of this particular EI component, it's good news for us that it's never too early to start teaching your children to be emotionally literate. From the time that children demonstrate verbal abilities, they can be taught how to label, communicate, and manage their feelings. Though we can continue to teach our children the value of emotional comprehension and management throughout their lives, those early years are especially important. When children are young, they absorb everything around them and use every experience to learn. If we make use of this in the right way, we can ensure that our children are equipped with all the skills and knowledge they need to live happy, fulfilled lives.

Naturally, we can't teach our children everything they would ever need to know all at once. Rather, we can stagger the learning process by instilling them with certain values and skills. At some ages, this learning will be easier as well as more applicable. At other times, you may find your parenting journey suddenly traveling uphill. But that's a bridge you can cross when you get there. For now, let's take a look at which things we can teach our kids and at what age we can do so.

Under Three Years Old

In the first three years of life, emotional literacy should focus on cultivating emotional language. At this stage, children are slowly starting to learn how to use and understand language. However, their emotions don't start when they are able to string words together. As such, it's important for you to help them develop this emotional language so that they are able to understand their feelings and verbalize them accurately. Creating this sort of language is relatively easy. It starts with you and the labeling of your own emotions. Remember how observant kids are at this age? Use that to your advantage by clueing your child in as to what the emotions are that they see in you and others in their life. Next, you can allow your children to attach words to their own emotions by labeling what they feel as you see it. When they're laughing, tell them that it's a sign of happiness. With enough repetition, they will form a connection between the word and the sensation (Raising Children Network (Australia), 2022).

From Three to Eight Years Old

Once your children have a firm grasp on the basics of verbal communication as well as the human experience in general, their emotional education takes a proactive turn. In the five years between the ages of three and eight, our children will increasingly practice the naming and expression of their feelings. However, our responsibility as emotionally intelligent parents is to ensure that they can do so easily. The only surefire way to do so is to ensure that they identify and work through emotions before they become too intense. Between these two ages, kids are still playing quite often, and much of their emotional learning can take place during playtime when they are free to explore and experiment. However, if they are upset or overwhelmed, they will be unable to effectively manage their emotions, and things may get worse for them on the inside.

For this part of their lives, your emotional literacy teachings can start with recognition and comprehension before moving on to management (Raising Children Network (Australia), 2022). You will have to engage with your child's emotions as much as you can and help them see that having feelings is normal. You can do this by linking their emotional experiences to those of the characters in their favorite book, show, or film. Remember that you are still the most impactful behavioral model. Tell your kids how you go about identifying your emotions, and have them use a similar technique to understand their own. You can also expand their comprehension by asking them how certain feelings manifest physically. Finally, help them understand their emotions by using the thing they like to do most: play. Create a relaxed environment in which the both of you can have some fun and explore your inner states. Play a round of emotional charades to help them understand how different feelings may look in different people.

Once you've done this, you can start teaching them coping skills. This can be anything from mindfulness exercises to the creation of a reaction system. With the former, they can move away from the distress of powerful, negative emotions. With the latter, they will have a go-to means of expression for both good and bad emotions. As you teach them, make sure that you let them know how natural it is to feel something and express it. Additionally, make sure that they understand that while emotional expression is natural and healthy, explosive behavior must be avoided.

Values to Instill in Your Child by Age Five

As we make our way along this road of emotional education, we must make a quick pit stop at the halfway point in our child's first decade on Earth. By the age of five, our children ought to be adopting a number of values that will form part of their core beliefs, which in turn will act as their moral and emotional guides through life. These values, along with the emotional skills they have learned by this age, will help our children form a concrete sense of self, one that will help them along their way to success in life, whatever it may be.

First and foremost: honesty. By teaching children the value of transparency and openness, you teach them the value of integrity, which will help them weather the social storm that comes with entering the school years. When children enter new environments, they may make mistakes more often. This is entirely natural, but the fear of getting in trouble due to missteps may lead children to start lying. To prevent this, make sure that honesty is instilled in your child by actively listening to them, creating a space in which they can safely share their emotions, and ensuring that they will not be punished for coming clean. Teach your children that, while they will have to face the consequences of their actions, honesty in and of itself won't get them into trouble.

Along with honesty, children will benefit from learning the values of sharing and cooperation. By teaching them this, you prepare them for the transactional and collaborative nature of interpersonal interactions. Once you have these two values down pat, you can move on to respect. This particular value is high on just about every parent's list of things they wish for their children to learn. The best way for you to raise a respectful child is to model this behavior yourself. Consider how you interact with others and what this shows your child. When demonstrating respect in your own encounters, explain to your child why this value is essential and what you do to show it. Along with the many other positives attached to respect through its acquisition, children learn the importance of diversity when it comes to opinions, beliefs, and backgrounds (Welch, 2018).

Other values your child will be able to handle by the age of five include kindness and making amends. The former helps them retain a state of emotional calm and control even when faced with the nastiness of the world. The latter teaches them accountability as well as how to admit when they have made a mistake and face its consequences. Alongside these values, five-year-olds should learn the power of forgiveness as well as the importance of considering others. Both of these values will teach them the validity of their feelings while demonstrating how they should handle the actions of others. Along with these, you can teach your child gratitude so that they may have a more positive outlook on life and learn to cope with anxiety.

We conclude this section on the past half-decade by looking at one final value: perseverance. You must teach your children how to push through tough times in order to reach their goals. In order to do this, you have to let go of the reins a bit and allow them to take responsibility for and control certain aspects of their lives. Moreover, you don't need to heap praise on each and every one of their efforts. Instead, teach them that they should be proud of the fact that they tried and that it is okay to fail. When your child does succeed, remind them that they achieved their goal through tenacity and dedication and that they are more than capable of doing so again.

Values to Instill in Your Child by Age 10

By the time your child reaches the end of their first, most formative decade, the values that form part of their emotional literacy should have grown in number. On your part as a parent, this may prove to be a difficult task, especially if we consider the importance of these values to a child's overall emotional intelligence. However, the silver lining around this specific child-rearing cloud is that you can teach these values steadily over those first 10 years. Your child doesn't have to adopt each of these emotional skills overnight. You can consider what they already know, gauge what they are ready for, and work from there.

In addition to building on the values taught during the first five years, the latter five can be used to add some new layers to enrich and enhance your child's emotional life. The first of these new values is accountability, which will help your kids determine the direction their everyday lives will take. By 10, children are well acquainted with the workings of the school environment, where they exist without the guidance of their parents. Here, they must consider their own behavior as well as the consequences attached to their actions. By teaching your children to be accountable, you enable them to also engage in some introspection on a larger scale. If they are unhappy with the results of their behavior and know to look inward to find its origins, they will examine their value system and make the necessary adjustments.

This last aspect of accountability goes hand-in-hand with curiosity. As irksome as your child's questions may sometimes be, the fact that they ask them is a good thing. Help your child explore the world of emotions by talking about your own values and why you hold them. Ask them what they believe and why they think the way they do. Much like accountability, this will provide them with an opportunity for introspection. What they learn about themselves may just motivate them to keep up a healthy sense of inquisitiveness as they move forward in life.

Our second-to-last value of the decade is tied very closely to the concept of EI as a whole. Learning the skill of empathy is essential to the establishment of significant, healthy relationships. When we teach our children to be more empathetic, we are opening their eyes to just how far-reaching the impact of their emotions stretches. At this age, children will have the idea that their feelings influence more people than just themselves. However, by teaching empathy, children learn to manage their emotions in such a way that they may be of use to others. This can aid them in everything from making new friends to resolving conflict (Welch, 2018). Teaching a concept as nebulous as empathy may prove difficult. As such, try to integrate these lessons into times when your child is relaxed and happy. They will be more receptive to your input in these moments and will be able to process at least the very basic aspects of this value.

Finally, the pedagogy of the first decade comes to an end with a value that demonstrates its value when practically applied. By the age of 10, our children should be able to communicate openly and honestly. If they are able to express what they feel, they will also be able to tell you about their desires and needs. In a demonstration of a uniquely positive domino effect, this, in turn, will strengthen the parent-child bond. Additionally, open communication is the bedrock of a healthy relationship and will come in handy in just about every connection your child makes in their life. When teaching them how to express themselves effectively, it is important that you take their personality into account. Some children will be comfortable speaking plainly from the start, while others may prefer more subtle means of communication. Find what works for your child, and help them nurture and develop their method.

Emotional Literacy for Pre-Teens and Teenagers

There is perhaps no period in life when emotions are felt quite as strongly as in the final years of childhood. As our children begin to change and become adolescents, their internal states are thrown into turmoil. I'm sure I don't need to remind you that this experience only intensifies in the teenage years when nothing that has happened or ever will happen can rival the feelings of your teen in that specific moment. However, just because our children suddenly possess this wealth of emotion doesn't mean they know what to do with any of it.

This is where you come in. During these years of your child's life, it's important that your parenting tactics become proactive. You have to pay attention to your child so that you can spot when their emotional state changes. When you have observed these changes, you can step in and help them work through whatever it is they are experiencing. At this age, emotional literacy focuses mostly on teaching your child the same proactive skills you use as a parent. Talk to them about becoming emotionally self-aware. Show them how you identify the signs of your own strong emotions and help them build their own system for observation.

Make sure that these skills are comprehensive so that they can see the physical as well as the behavioral changes. Help your child build and hone this set of skills by compiling them into a list. Use trial and error to see what works, and use these tactics to help them make it through those rough adolescent waters. Speaking of rough times, if you can't step in before your child's emotions become too much, give them space to work through what they feel. Once they have returned to their typical emotional state, sit down with them and go over what they felt, how they handled it, and how they view their experience of their emotions now.

Practicing What You Preach: How to Be an Emotionally Intelligent Parent

One of the most impactful things you can do as an emotionally intelligent parent is to put your tactics into practice. We know by now that so much of what our child uses to construct their identity comes from the behavior we model for them. As such, the best way we can ensure that our children lean into the power of their EI is by showing them how to do so. Demonstrating how to be emotionally intelligent can be done in a variety of ways. In keeping with the theme of making adjustments to your particular parenting situation, consider adopting those practices and behaviors that suit you, your circumstances, and your family best.

Taking Care of Yourself

Like so many other aspects of parenthood, living an emotionally intelligent life begins with you and the way you treat yourself. You can't very well expect your children to be kind to themselves and take care of themselves if they see you doing the opposite. Learn to be kind to yourself and to accept the reality of who you are. It can be easy to lose sight of your own needs and well-being once you become a parent. This is especially true in those early years when just about every waking moment is spent making sure your child is okay. However, these years are among the most important, as children observe and absorb everything you say and do. As such, make sure that you pay attention to your own emotional state, fulfill your needs, and do whatever it is you need to take care of yourself. Not only will you be more in control of your feelings, but you will also become a more alert and attentive parent.

Recognizing the Obstacles in Your Way

In an ideal world, you'd start parenting at birth and just sail right through to the day your children become independent, fully-rounded adults. We can only dream. The reality is much different, and you may encounter many obstacles on the path towards raising a child with a strong EI. The obstacles you encounter will sometimes be specific to your circumstances, but there are a few of these difficulties that are more common than others. As you learn how to model EI for your children, consider that you might encounter any of the following:

- Modern society's overemphasis on mental intelligence over emotional insight. We have discussed this to some extent already, but it is worth mentioning again. Many of the role players in your child's life, i.e., teachers, friends, etc., will tell you that the only knowledge that matters is that which can be applied in the classroom. We know this to be patently untrue, so stick to your guns and push for your child to focus on developing their EI.

- The disconnection you may sometimes feel from your own emotions. Parenting is a difficult and demanding endeavor that often takes up nearly all of our mental and emotional resources. Similar to the way in which you must care for yourself, you must make sure that you stay in touch with your feelings if you are in touch with them but are unsure of how to work through or manage them, try any of the strategies we have explored thus far to see how you can build and strengthen this connection.

- Constant preoccupation. We don't parent in a vacuum, and we often find ourselves juggling work at home with work at the office. Rushing from one task to the next may often lead to us ignoring our emotional needs because we just don't have the time.

- The busy nature of our lives might lead us to focus on tasks whose results we can easily see and quantify. Given how abstract emotions are, we tend to neglect work in this area because we can't physically or immediately see the progress we make.

- A lack of emotional knowledge stems from childhood. If our parents didn't model emotionally intelligent behavior for us, it could be difficult to build this practice from scratch. Sometimes, this difficulty may stem from unresolved emotional issues from childhood.

We may repress some difficult or painful experiences, which will complicate things for us in the present.

- External sources tell us that EI isn't essential to the parenting process. Much of today's parenting literature focuses more on the positives and negatives of children's behavior. These sources examine behavior on the surface alone and seek to fix actions without examining the emotions that motivate them.

- Most of us may be aware of what we think of ourselves, but we are unaware of how others perceive us. This lack of self-awareness directly prevents us from accessing one of the core tenets of EI.

- The primal aspect of emotions may interfere with logical processes. Sometimes, we react instinctively without considering the consequences, which may prove detrimental to our attempts at emotional management.

Follow the Rules You Set

Though this may seem obvious, it is essential. Your children may sometimes question the rules and boundaries you establish. By following the guidelines you construct, explaining the reasoning behind them, and demonstrating their positive effects, you show your children that the household rules work to their benefit. In turn, you may find your discipline strategies becoming more effective and being accepted with less resistance (Morin, 2018).

Place Emphasis on Connection

We already know that establishing a meaningful connection with your child is essential to our purpose here. However, you can be an emotionally intelligent parent without telling your child that you are working on this bond. All you have to do is ensure that your child feels supported, safe, seen, and heard. Additionally, you can make them feel loved by engaging with their interests, establishing rituals you can do together, and taking the time to do something special. None of these have to be huge events; it's the sentiment that matters.

Focus on the Motivation Inherent in Your Child's Mind

Singhal (2021) defines the concept of intrinsic motivation as "the ability to persist and continue with a task despite obstacles and without seeking others' approval." You can help your child develop this part of themselves by showing them how to set goals and brainstorming ways they can achieve them. In doing so, ensure that you teach them that it is the process and dedication that matter, not the extent to which they achieve success. Support them in their pursuits, but allow them to try as much as they can on their own.

Never Forget the Importance of Values

We've already covered some of the values you can teach throughout childhood. Some of the practical ways in which you can impart this wisdom include:

- Relate it to your child's experiences and the world in which they live.

- Take care to make them aware of your behavior and values, as this is what you model for them.

- Take time to discuss values with your children. Explain to them what yours are, why you hold them, and what they mean to you.

- Explain the role that values play in motivating your behavior.

- Talk to your children about how you describe your values as well as how you express them. Make sure to teach them about the habits you adopt to facilitate this expression.

- Resist the urge to lecture them about values. Instead, facilitate open and honest communication. It is essential that this conversation be a dialogue as opposed to a few minutes in which you talk to your children.

- Get involved in your community by reaching out to those in need and doing your bit for charity.

- Include your children in community service by signing up as a family. Involve them in the decision-making process when you decide on a cause or organization to support.

- Allow your child the opportunity to express altruism on their own, without your influence or guidance. Encourage them to make contributions or volunteer. You can help them to an extent, but you must allow them the space to apply this value on their own.

- Discuss the role that money plays in modern society and emphasize the importance of understanding its function. If applicable, discuss the way in which your culture or community views money and how it influences your values and behaviors.

- Choose literature and media you can engage with alongside your child that will allow you to start a discussion about values. Regardless of whether the piece aligns with your values, discuss your experience with and interpretation of it. You can also tell your kids about an instance in your day where you had to exercise judgment regarding your values. Tell them about your thought process and ask for their input.

- Teach them how to navigate relationships, conflict, and competition through the concept of good sportsmanship.

- Instill values tied to morality by explaining that, despite the difficulty that may come with doing the right thing, its effects are what must motivate us to do it. We must believe that when we do good, some part of the universe is changed or improved. Despite the fact that we can't prove it, it is this hope that we must use to keep us tied to our values.

Put in the Work

There are a massive number of things in life for which your children will have to work. You can prepare them for this by teaching them how to have a strong work ethic. Regardless of what you do, whether at home or at your workplace, make sure that your children see your efforts. Talk to them about the satisfaction and fulfillment you get from doing work, and hear their thoughts on the matter as well. A practical way to teach them the value of work is through performing chores together. Large or small, the sense of achievement these tasks will give them will contribute to the acquisition of this particular attribute.

Adopt the Practice of Emotion Coaching

Emotion coaching can be defined as "being [clued] into your child's (and your own) feelings, helping your child identify and name their feelings, and enabling emotional regulation" (Singhal, 2021). We will explore this practice in more depth in just a moment. For now, know that you can use it to teach your kids that while all their emotions are valid, not all their expressions may be appropriate. Applying emotion coaching methods will help you and your children develop valuable coping mechanisms and strategies.

Emotion Coaching

We already have a basic understanding of what emotion coaching is, but to fully comprehend it, we must examine its practical aspects as well. From an actionable point of view, this practice is all about teaching your children how to recognize their emotions and subsequently helping them construct mechanisms for control and regulation (Li, 2021). Emotion coaching involves a measure of mindfulness as children become more aware of their own emotions and the emotions of others in their lives, as well as the appropriate way to approach and deal with these feelings. Essentially, you are teaching your child how healthy human emotion is so that they may develop the skills they need to succeed.

Coaching as Opposed to Dismissing

Sometimes, we parents tend to be dismissive of our children's emotional experiences. In some cases, this is intentional, as parents feel frustrated with their child's inability to cope with these feelings on their own. At other times, this dismissal comes from the parent being overwhelmed by everything else going on in life and simply not having the emotional bandwidth to handle the situation carefully and considerately. Regardless of its origins, dismissing your child's feelings really isn't the way to go.

By not engaging with our children's experiences, we are not only modeling unhealthy attitudes regarding expression but are actively harming our children. When they are dismissed, children get the impression that sharing their emotions is bad or unwanted. Moreover, by denying them the space and time in which to work through whatever it is they are feeling, you may be worsening your child's emotional state. If this doesn't happen, they may decide to repress their emotions, which will certainly come back to haunt all of you at some point down the line.

What you must do instead is adopt the coaching approach. Crucially, we must understand that switching from dismissing to coaching doesn't mean that we suddenly take control of our children's emotions. Though we will be actively engaging with them in times of distress, our influence is slightly more indirect as we provide our kids with the tools they need to become emotionally self-sufficient. In addition to the positive effects that this approach has on our children, we may find ourselves viewing their emotions and behaviors more positively. By taking the time to teach our children these skills, we are fostering a closer bond with them, helping them avoid the pitfalls and dangers of emotional development, and creating a more positive environment in which they can flourish (Katz & Gottman, 1997).

Why Should You Practice Emotion Coaching?

In addition to those benefits already identified, the greatest argument for emotion coaching can be found in its link to success. Though our focus is on EQ, it's still worth noting that children who demonstrate a degree of emotional self-regulation are academically strong. If we look for something more in line with our purposes here, we see that these same children have been observed to have a greater capacity for socialization and demonstrate stronger social skills. We must also consider what emotional coaching steers our children away from. By learning how to control and regulate their emotional states, they lower their risk of developing mental health problems, specifically emotional and personality disorders (Li, 2021).

When we lead our children through the process of emotion coaching, we are helping them to understand not only the importance of their feelings but also how they can make the most of their power. All-in-all, the most compelling argument that emotion coaching makes for its practice is the fact that, when you pool all its effects together, what you end up doing is strengthening your child's EI and therefore raising their EQ.

The Steps of Emotion Coaching

If the payoff of this practice has intimidated you somewhat, rest assured that its actual implementation is an absolute piece of cake. Adopting emotion coaching practices can be done in five easy steps.

Understand Your Current Approach to Emotions

Before you can help your child gain control of their emotional state, it's imperative that you first understand how you react to their emotions now. The better you understand your current approach, the better you will be able to construct your new method. In addition to determining how you look at emotions, you must also figure out where your perspective comes from.

As part of this process, examine your childhood, the way your parents responded to your emotions and the way you think of your feelings in adulthood. Though you can tailor the questions you ask yourself to be more specific to your circumstances, use the following as an indication of how they ought to look:

- Behaviorally, how did your parents respond to your emotional expression?

- When you expressed how you felt, how much support were you given, and how understanding were your parents?

- When you think of being confronted with someone else's distress, how would you react? Do you believe that you could provide helpful guidance or facilitate problem-solving?

- Do you think of strong emotions (positive or negative) as self-indulgent and unproductive, or that they get in the way of things such as productivity and focus?

- When you become upset, what do you do to help yourself calm down? Do you work through what you feel, or do you compartmentalize and move on?

See Emotions as Opportunities for Learning and Growth

Don't approach your child's moments of expression from a place of logic. Instead, when those negative feelings make their presence known, sit down with your child and have a talk. Help them verbalize what they feel, label the sensation, and allow them the space to explain the ins and outs of their experience. In doing so, you model empathetic behavior for your child and teach them how to be an active listener.

By giving your child the opportunity to feel what they feel in a safe environment, you teach them that feeling is important. However, by talking through and labeling their emotions, your child will understand their feelings better. At the end of it all, they realize that while all they feel is valid, not all of their reactions and behaviors are equally okay. This is especially true of negative emotions, which you must be sure to address from a problem-solving perspective as well.

Practice Empathy and Validation

Encourage your child to share their feelings with you. When they do so, make sure that you engage in active and empathetic listening. This means that you take control of each of your senses, focus them on the present as your child sits in front of you, and take in all that they are sharing with you. Once they have said their piece, reassure them that their feelings are valid, as are the outcomes they tie to their experiences. Conclude this step by teaching them self-regulation by recognizing that the behaviors that result from their feelings aren't always okay, even if they are allowed to feel whatever they like.

Label Their Emotions

For many children, their lack of understanding is what contributes most to their experiences of emotional distress. When your child describes their inner state, help them attach a name to that sensation. The simple act of naming something will already enhance their sense of control. For this step, it is essential that you label what they really feel, not the emotion you think they should achieve after this experience. Moreover, help them understand that their emotions aren't set in stone. While the word "angry" may feel appropriate right now, the more they examine their feelings, they might find that "irritated" is a better fit.

Follow Through

Much of your time spent on emotion coaching will be focused on the resolution of negative emotions and problems. Naturally, you will be constructing your own version of the following through. For reference, have a look at the following strategies:

- Establish boundaries and limits concerning emotionally-driven or reactive behavior.

- Follow through on your parenting tactics by enforcing rules and maintaining household boundaries. When your child misbehaves, allow for the appropriate consequences to be felt so that they may learn the impact of their actions.

- Along with your child, brainstorm actionable solutions that will help them regulate their emotions. Work out what these solutions will be, as well as the steps you and your child will take to see them through.

Dos and Don'ts

Chances are, emotion coaching will be something new you add to your parenting repertoire. Despite the fact that this practice is easy enough to pick up and integrate into your daily functioning, there are some things you should be aware of when first starting to coach your child. First and foremost, you have to remember that no two kids are alike. As such, if you are implementing this practice with more than one of your children, don't expect the same things to work for both of them and for one to respond in the same way as the other. This is perfectly fine, as each of your children will need coaching that speaks to their emotional needs and struggles.

Secondly, don't expect them to be able to pick up these skills after only one attempt. Remember that you are teaching your child behaviors and thought processes with which they aren't naturally born. Meet them on their level, and build your practices from there. Additionally, consider your child's emotional life as a whole and not as isolated instances of difficulty. Think back to when you were a kid and what you struggled with emotionally. Be proactive and have a plan ready for those obstacles, as it will make the coaching process much easier.

Finally, don't be afraid to say "no." As counterintuitive as it may seem, allowing your child the space and freedom to explore will be one of the most valuable experiences when it comes to learning emotional literacy (Talaris Institute, 2023). In the course of this exploration, they will make mistakes and find things that suit them well. Encourage them to learn from the former and praise them for supplementing their emotional state with the latter. Wherever you can, make the emotion coaching process as collaborative and fun as you can. The more invested you appear to your child, the more profound the effects of this process will be.

Fun and Creative Ways to Teach Your Child Emotional Literacy

As parents, we know that children are more likely to remember something if it's presented to them in a fun way. By making emotional literacy an enjoyable experience, you allow your child to use more of their cognitive ability, which in turn will allow these experiences' lessons to stick in their minds. Before you explore this section further, note that you don't have to use all of the methods discussed. Instead, choose those that your child will respond to the most and integrate them into your approach.

Games

Games can be a fun way to teach emotional literacy and can even involve the entire family. When teaching your child EI skills, consider the following games:

- "Simon Says" with an EI twist: Put an emotionally literate spin on this classic game by changing the commands so that players act out different emotions. For older kids, you can add a layer of effort by instructing them to act out their reactions to situations as well. You can work on your own EI using this game by having a round or two where you demonstrate your own emotions to show your kids what you'd like them to imitate.

- Emotional charades: This game is perfect for the whole family. You can start easily by having team members act out basic emotions. As the game progresses, change the prompts to scenarios in which your kids will have to act out emotionally intelligent responses and behaviors.

- Guess my emotion: This is also a variation of a game night staple. Write down a bunch of emotions on some cards, shuffle the cards, and choose one. Making sure you can't see the emotion on your selected card, hold it up to your forehead. You can also attach it to your head with a rubber band if you prefer. Subsequently, your child will have to describe the emotion on your card, after which you will do the same for the feeling on their forehead. You can also elevate this game by constructing scenarios for your child to describe, as they will employ their EI and demonstrate their emotional reasoning process while doing so.

Activities

Similar to emotional literacy games, you can undertake these activities alone with your child or make it a family effort:

- Journaling: This activity may be solitary in execution, but you can encourage your whole family to take part. If your child has never journaled before, show them how to go about it. Encourage them to write down everything they felt during the day and how well they believe they handled it. It's important that you don't force your child to share with you what they have written in their journal. Rather, remind them that they can tell you if they want. Regardless of their decision, check in regularly to see how the journaling process is going and discuss what they feel they have learned through it.

- Emotionally-oriented people-watching: This one might sound weird, but bear with me. When you are out and about with your child and the two of you have a moment, take a look at the people around you. Ask your child what they think those people are feeling. Ask them for specifics and to provide more details than merely "happy" or "angry." Have them provide motivations for their answers so that both of you can learn about their interpretation of visual markers of emotions. If doing this in public isn't your thing, take a magazine and try it out on the photos. You can even perform this exercise while watching television with your child (more on that below).

- Emotional labeling: This activity is incredibly simple. All it involves is you sitting down with your child and starting a conversation centered around the phrase "I am feeling…" Doing this will provide both of you with a safe space in which to express your emotions. If your child is struggling to verbalize their feelings, or if you want to add an element of fun, you can try to guess what they are feeling. For this, use the phrase "I wonder if you're feeling…" Phrasing it this way prevents you from leading your child to any specific emotion and lets them know how their expression comes across to other people.

Visual Aids

Some children respond better to images than instructions. This approach is relatively easy, as there is a legion of YouTube videos out there that help your child learn skills linked to emotional literacy. If you want something more personal for your child, consider combining their favorite film or television show with the people-watching activity. You can pause the visual aid at any point and ask your child to identify the characters' emotions in that scene. You can also do this at the end of the runtime and ask your child which emotions they remember most vividly. Rewind to those scenes so that they can have a visual aid to help them describe the emotion more expansively. You can also use the visual stimulation to ask your child how the emotions on screen make them feel in that moment.

You can also create or buy something like an emotion wheel or cards depicting certain feelings. Sit your child down for an open discussion about emotions. When they falter or feel unsure, use these visual aids to help them identify the image that most closely reflects their emotional state in that moment. With the emotion identified, continue the conversation to build upon its understanding.

Role Play

This particular exercise is similar to the emotional charades you can play. The key difference, however, is that you don't have to adhere to the nonverbal rules of the classic game. Instead, you can construct a few different scenarios that you and your child can act out and work through. If you're not sure where to start, refer back to Chapter 1 and build five separate scenarios, each linked to one of the aspects of emotional intelligence. This way, you will cover the very basics, take note of your child's strengths and weaknesses, and adjust your next game to help them in these areas. Alternatively, ask for your child's input and put together scenarios based on emotions, situations, or interactions they find difficult. Take turns inhabiting the roles of each person concerned. In doing so, you will see the level of EI your child is operating at and subsequently model a healthy response for them.

Toys

What child doesn't love a good toy? Though some may be bought, you can make a few of these toys at home, which may be preferable as you can customize them for your child:

- Clay: Use this toy in a session of informally structured play. Give your child a prompt consisting of an emotion, simple or complex. Ask them to represent this emotion in clay. What they build can reflect their interpretation of the emotion or can take shape as something they associate with that emotional experience, for example, a person, place, or object.

- Feelings jar: This toy is more of a long-term asset to have around the house. Moreover, there are variations of this jar you can use. You can make or buy one that has 365 individual cards, each with a different emotion or experience on it. These jars have a card you can draw on each day of the year with the intention of engaging with your child about that day's emotion. Another variant is used on a more contextual basis. The contents are the same, although the cards aren't necessarily meant to be used each day. Instead, your child can select a card that reflects their emotional state at that time. You then sit with them and work through the experience, perhaps drawing a card that might better describe their feelings or that is related to it. This process helps them learn about their emotional expression as well as the complexity of feelings.

Emotion Coaching Phrases

Emotion coaching is all about feedback and fostering open communication with your child. As with the techniques used to teach emotional literacy, your method of emotion coaching must be tailored to your child's needs and capabilities. Use the expressions listed below as inspiration for the phrases you will employ whenever a teachable moment presents itself.

- It's alright to feel bad and to express those emotions.

- Things may be bad right now, but this feeling won't last forever.

- Take a step back, breathe, and think.

- I'm always here if you need me.

- You won't have to work through this alone. I'm here for you.

- You don't have to talk about it right now; we can do that whenever you are ready.

- What you are feeling is valid, but do you think the way you reacted was equally okay?

- What do you think you can learn from this experience?

- Don't worry; we all make mistakes. You'll remember that for the next time.

- I'm sorry; I misunderstood you. Let's start from the beginning.

The strategies outlined in this chapter are enough to put you firmly on your way towards raising your child to be emotionally strong and healthy. As you attempt these techniques, remember that this is very much a team effort, one aimed at development and change. If you hope to succeed and to set your child up for success in turn, you must turn your intentions towards growth and change. Given enough time and practice, your entire household will be a well-oiled, emotionally literate machine.

Chapter 4:

The Growth Mindset for

Growing Minds

Don't worry about failure. Worry about the chances you miss when you don't even try. –Jack Canfield

Helping your child through the different stages of emotional development can be a daunting prospect, especially if we consider all the other changes they are constantly experiencing. Childhood is a time of constant evolution as your child grows into the person they were meant to be. Sometimes, this change can be overwhelming, and you may encounter some resistance to the idea of focusing on EI. Your child may want to focus on those intelligences that are regarded as more important by society. Their resistance may also come from something as simple as difficulty.

This is understandable, as no one becomes emotionally intelligent overnight. However, it is in these moments that you must remind your child that there is immense power to be found in the concept of "yet." Yes, they may not have all the tools and knowledge they need, but crucially, they don't have them yet. With a bit of practice and open-mindedness, there's no reason why they shouldn't achieve all they desire. The first step towards doing this is changing your perspective on the strengthening of EI by adopting something we are increasingly encountering in popular psychology: the growth mindset.

What Is a Growth Mindset?

Simply put, a growth mindset is a belief in your own ability to change and improve. If we elaborate on that, we find that it involves believing that you can build your skills and intelligence through things like commitment, effort, accountability, and facing challenges head-on (Yacoub, 2021). The concept of the growth mindset was first conceptualized by American psychologist Carol Dweck. Her work has provided us with most of the language we use nowadays when discussing success, motivation, and stagnation related to our emotions and behaviors.

Dweck's original concept of a growth mindset requires a person to view their innate abilities and predispositions as a sort of jumping-off point. While the things you are naturally good at are certainly admirable, you should take stock of them to determine where you are now and then build your personal development from there. It is essential to understand that, for people with a growth mindset, improvement and development are the most important things. Though they may aim for it, absolute perfection isn't the metric for success. Instead, they look at the effort put in and the progress they have made. If they have changed or strengthened something, it's a job well done. There will always be room for improvement, but a growth mindset allows you to be content with working towards being the best and knowing that you will get there someday.

Since its introduction into the popular consciousness some two decades ago, the concept of a growth mindset has become an increasingly popular tool for individuals and organizations alike. However, as with most things that are disseminated among the public, there are some misconceptions that can pop up now and again. It's important that we address these before we move forward so that we have a clear idea of what to expect when starting to adopt this mindset for ourselves and our children.

Firstly, hard work does not mean constant work. This mindset does encourage us to seek out opportunities for self-improvement and to believe that we are never incapable of change. This does not mean that we must be working on ourselves 24/7. Many people believe that to have a growth mindset, one must never stop working. This misconception is as dangerous as it is incorrect. The surge in growth mindset adoption over the last few years has fed into the concept of "grind culture," which dictates that your entire life should revolve around working, improving, and developing. This, however, leads to burnout and other physical and mental health issues (Cornwall, 2022). Pacing your development is more than fine, and knowing when to take a step back and slow down doesn't mean your belief in yourself has diminished; it just means you are self-aware enough to make that call.

Secondly, it's crucial to understand that adopting this mindset is a conscious decision you make. While some people innately possess an open-minded, flexible, and adaptable disposition, this isn't entirely the same. A growth mindset may involve building on these qualities, but it also involves actively choosing to adopt practices and habits that allow you to move away from the rigidity of a fixed mindset, which we will explore in a moment. Some people may learn quicker than others, but no one just falls into this mindset. It takes work and dedication. Luckily, these are two things to which a growth mindset helps you become more open.

The last thing we ought to clear up is the level of praise and reward that comes with growth mindsets and parenting. While it's important that we don't fixate on how much success our child achieves, it's also important that we make sure they know their efforts ought to amount to something. Encourage them to grow and develop but ensure that they have a goal or end result in mind. Effort for effort's sake doesn't help anyone and may lead to your child sustaining work beyond their limits because they haven't established what it is they wish to achieve with their newfound growth mindset.

Through Dweck's exploration of human motivation and perspective, she came to define two separate mindsets. The first, the growth mindset, is one we have already encountered and one we must attempt to teach our children. The other, the fixed mindset, is diametrically opposite to the first and focuses on a person's inability to change. Though this mindset might sound harmful (it is), understanding it helps us learn what a growth mindset is not and what to avoid in the teaching process.

The best definition of the fixed mindset can be pulled from the book that originated these concepts, in which it is defined as a perspective of "you have it, or you don't" (Dweck, 2006). This characteristic is also what sets this mindset apart from its growth-oriented counterpart. Where people with a growth mindset see failures as opportunities for learning and adjustment, a fixed mindset invites a more all-or-nothing outlook. If they can't achieve something, they are inclined to believe that they are inherently incapable of it. This mindset can be incredibly detrimental, as people who have this fixed perspective believe that they must prove themselves at every turn. If they fail to do so, it must mean that they just can't do it and that that particular skill will elude them forever.

A fixed mindset is what is holding a lot of us, and many of our children, back from achieving our goals. This perspective on life sees each person cast in stone, stagnating everything from their skill set to their personality to their objectives in life. As part of our journey towards a state of elevated EI, we must let go of the idea of such inflexible limitations and learn to embrace our malleability and all the potential that comes along with it. There is so much all of us can achieve; we just haven't done it yet.

The Importance of the Growth Mindset

Apart from making our children more receptive to the acquisition of new skills and knowledge, developing a growth mindset feeds into certain aspects of emotional intelligence.

The first of these aspects is motivation, primarily because this mindset fuels your child and changes the way they think of motivation as a whole. Before, your child may have had motivational tunnel vision, where the only thing driving them was the achievement of their desired end result. While this is certainly an important part of motivation, a growth mindset enables your child to expand its components to include an appreciation for the learning opportunity that trying brings. Children with this mindset recognize that a goal is important but that there are many lessons to be learned along the way as well (Williams, 2018). Each of these lessons will help them understand themselves, their purpose, and their world more profoundly. Moreover, this mindset fuels a child's curiosity, cultivates a hunger for learning, and enables them to develop their problem-solving skills.

A growth mindset is important for our specific purposes here, as this perspective on life sets our children up for success throughout life. They become more world-savvy, learning that life can often be difficult and that their attempts may not always succeed the first time around. This realization may make them more self-aware and open their eyes to their strengths and weaknesses. Subsequently, they will know which areas of development to focus on in order to grow. Perhaps most important of all, a growth mindset is something that a person works at for life. As such, the improvements to their EI they gain in childhood will carry them for years, changing and adapting right along with them.

From a practical point of view, adopting a growth mindset helps your child become more resilient and teaches them the skill of perseverance. This is where our role as parents comes in quite significantly. You see, this particular benefit is contingent on the language we use in connection with intelligence—both emotional and academic. We teach our children these qualities by knowing when to motivate them and to what extent. We've already covered this in part in the previous section, where we talked about the importance of working towards a specific goal. But it's equally important to let your children know that their efforts are admirable and that even if they fail, they ought to be proud that they tried. By attaching meaning to the process, you teach your kids to strengthen their resolve and push through until they get to the destination they have in mind (Williams, 2018).

How to Help Your Child Develop Their Growth Mindset

Naturally, your children won't just magically open up their minds to the possibility and potential of growth. It's up to you as the parent to help them with this cerebral and emotional expansion, as well as help them cope with all that goes along with it. There are a number of simple things you can do to help your child break free from the restrictions of a fixed mindset.

Focus on the Process

When you first start teaching your child to have a growth mindset, try verbalizing the importance of the process. If it seems like this point is getting a bit repetitive, it should be noted that it is massively important to success in this endeavor. Provide your child with as much positive, constructive feedback as you can. Acknowledge how much work they put in, regardless of the result. Additionally, make a point of remarking how impressed you are by their determination, especially given the difficulty of the task or activity. In doing so, you teach them that the development of problem-solving skills is what's important. This way, if your child isn't naturally adept at these types of things, they won't get discouraged and will learn the value of pushing through (Mangrum, 2021).

Use Failure as an Example

Speaking of trying but not always succeeding, help your child understand what a growth mindset looks like by using other people's failures and mistakes as an example. Crucially, choose people who did not give up when they encountered failure. The examples can be anyone, from famous people you know your child likes to family members or friends. Discuss with your child how these people didn't just fall into the success they enjoy but rather attained it through continued effort combined with trial and error. Make sure your child knows it's okay to stumble and even fall down. What matters is that they get up and move to the other side of the road before moving on.

Work With Your Child's Learning Style

If we consider that empowering our children with a growth mindset means teaching them certain skills, it stands to reason that we should do what we can to make the educational process as easy as possible. To do this, we have to establish what our child's learning style is and then tailor their emotional education to suit the way they learn. In general, a child's learning style refers to the way in which they process and retain information for later use (Cinelli, 2023). Thus far, four individual learning styles have been identified. They are:

- Visual, in which a child learns best using visual aids and stimuli.

- Tactile, in which a child learns through physical stimulation and touch.

- Auditory, in which a child learns through aural aids and stimuli.

- Kinesthetic, in which a child learns by using their physicality, doing activities, and moving around.

It can be difficult to know which style is most suited to your child. We must understand that when a particular style delivers the best results for your child, this is linked to their natural predisposition. If you hope to use this in the process of teaching your child, you have to understand that you can't impart the lessons according to the style that suits you best, nor can you try to teach your child a new style altogether. There's a reason why they are suited to these styles and not the other way around. Find out which of the four learning styles works best, and use that one to help your kids learn about this mindset.

Making this determination can be done in a number of different ways, though the quickest and most reliable method is good old-fashioned observation. If you simply pay attention to your kids, particularly during unstructured free time or playtime, you will be able to pick up on what their style may be. You will be able to identify the stimuli towards which they gravitate and see how well they retain the information imparted by these same things. If you'd prefer to see your child's style applied more academically, perform this observation while they are completing schoolwork. Take note of the approach they use as well as how they structure the notes they make to help them memorize the work. Most importantly, don't tell your child to do it another way, even if you would. Let your child be themselves, and there's no end to what you can learn.

If you would like to perform a more hands-on exercise, you can try choosing a specific stimulus and seeing how they respond to it. A good tool to use for this would be a non-fiction book, preferably one with illustrations or diagrams. Work through the book with them and take note of how they respond to the activity of reading. If they jump in and take charge of reading themselves, you may have a tactile learner who responds to holding the material in their hands. If they skim the paragraphs and focus instead on the information to be gleaned from the images, consider visual learning. Should your child ask that you read the information to them instead, they may be suited to the auditory style. Finally, if they demonstrate retention and understanding through recreating or retelling parts of the book, kinesthetic learning may be right up their alley. These are the same types of responses and behaviors you can look out for during observation as well.

Finally, you can gauge the style to which your child is suited by consulting professional resources. You can find an array of quizzes and assessments online that will help you do just that. Use any of these diagnostic tools in order to determine your child's learning style. For the most accurate results, have your child answer the questions themselves. You can even employ some observation here to see how they approach, and handle being tasked with a test. When you get the results, remember that children are complicated beings, and not everything about them can be perfectly quantified into separate categories. If the test determines that your child works with a combination of styles, use each of the styles mentioned to enhance their learning experience.

Lead by Example

We have already explored the impact that modeling behavior can have when trying to help your child work on their EI. When helping them develop a growth mindset, this impact remains just as potent (Yacoub, 2021). In this process, you have the chance to be emotionally intelligent yourself and foster honest communication with your child. Tell them about your perspective on your own ability to change and improve. Share with them the times you have faltered or failed and how you got yourself back on the path to success.

While talking and sharing may do the trick, there won't be anything quite as effective as a demonstration. Show your child how enriching it can be to learn a new skill or take on a fresh challenge. Remember to maintain a positive attitude as you embark on these new endeavors. Even when you fail, ensure that your child sees you trying again in order to demonstrate the learning process. If you'd like, include them in your activities where appropriate and take advantage of the added opportunity to strengthen your bond.

Rely on the Science

One way of ensuring your child can adopt a growth mindset is by explaining the validity of the practice. You can do this by discussing neuroplasticity with your children. Naturally, you don't have to go into extreme detail. At the very least, explain the concept of the plastic brain and how it is able to adapt throughout life. Explain to your child that this adaptation comes along with the formation of new neural pathways, which in turn help us adopt new behaviors as well as expand our cognitive functioning (Mangrum, 2021). If your child is relatively young or if you feel they won't grasp this concept, consider changing it into a metaphor. For instance, compared the human brain to a tree and those neural pathways to the roots branching off in search of nutrients and sustenance.

New Experiences

Growth mindsets are all about change and doing things that will help your child develop in new ways. You can do something stimulating, like puzzles, or get some endorphins flowing through exercise. Whatever you do, make sure that it sits anywhere other than in the dead center of your comfort zone. The more you explore, the better you will demonstrate to your child the potential that lies in adventure. The stronger the impact of this lesson, the greater the effect of a growth mindset will be in your child's life.

General Tips

In addition to those methods outlined above, you can keep the following in mind as you teach your child to become more adventurous, open, and flexible:

- Remember not to limit the impact of this mindset to learning new skills. Talk openly with your child about the ways in which a growth mindset can help them develop their EI, improve their performance at school, and just generally make them more prepared for life.

- Use appropriate language when teaching your child about this mindset. Be encouraging but not patronizing. Verbally reward them for their efforts and let them know you support their pursuits. However, it's crucial that you know where the line is between support and giving your kid-free rein.

- Don't shy away from being open about shortcomings, failures, and obstacles. Share these aspects of yourself so that your child is not only aware of the import of their humanity but also of the power to be found in embracing it.

Growth Mindset Activities

Now that you know how to go about teaching your child to have a growth mindset, you can practically implement this knowledge in a variety of activities. As with the approaches discussed in the previous section, you can use only those activities that would help your child the most. Feel free to alter their specifics to suit your child's emotional abilities and needs.

Attitude Transitions

This exercise is all about adjusting the way your child thinks about themselves and their capabilities. It teaches kids about the emotional language surrounding a growth mindset and the way they can take control of their inner voice, as well as negative self-talk.

Start this exercise by having your child make negative statements about themselves. Think along the lines of "I can't…," "I'm bad at…," and other things that hold them back. They can write down things they think about themselves, things others have said to them, and things they feel they will never achieve.

Once these sentences are finished, help your child transform them into positive, affirmative statements. Do this by replacing the negative, limiting words with those that encourage growth and development. By doing this, you are demonstrating that the capacity for change lies within them; all they have to do is unlock it.

Paper-Based Catharsis

This exercise is all about negative emotions and mistakes. More specifically, it's about letting them go and moving on. At the end of the week, have your child write down all the mistakes they made during those seven days. Additionally, they can write down all the negative emotions they felt during that same period. Ask them to be as specific as possible and to write each one down on a separate piece of paper. With all the mistakes and emotions written down, crumple up each piece of paper and throw it away. If you'd like, throw it at the wall.

Once you have thrown out all the papers, ask your child to pick them up and reopen them. Calmly and openly, discuss your child's experiences. Ask them how they think the mistakes happened, how they made your child feel, and what they would do to avoid making them again. If your child wrote down negative emotions, discuss these with them as well. Ask them what happened to elicit these feelings and how they responded in those situations. Encourage honest communication and give your child the space to construct their own solutions to the problems they face.

Building Self-Awareness

To help your child identify the parts of their life and personhood they can improve, help them construct a self-awareness checklist. Pose the questions listed below and ask them to write down detailed, honest answers. Once your child has all their answers, go over them together and construct a plan for the way forward.

- I think my strengths are…

- I think my weaknesses are…

- I feel the safest when…

- The thing that stresses me out the most is…

- Something I would love to achieve within the next year is…

- I think I need help with…

- The people I feel comfortable sharing my feelings with are…

Emotional Countdown

This exercise is also a tool for self-awareness and allows your child to take stock of their recent emotional behavior and change. You can start your countdown at any number. I would recommend opting for a healthy five. This number is small enough for young kids to handle, but it is also expansive enough to allow for a measure of meaningful reflection. Perform this exercise by having your child respond to the following five prompts:

- What are five good things that have happened in the last week?

- What are four things you think you can change in your life?

- What are three skills you have learned recently?

- What are two things you would like to do less of or remove from your life?

- What is the one positive change you believe you can make within the next week?

Scheduled Newness

We know that having new experiences is an integral part of adopting a growth mindset. However, actually getting around to these activities may prove difficult. Moreover, impulsively going on a new adventure may be fun and enriching, but its unpredictability can also prove detrimental. In order to avoid this, actively make time to have new experiences and to take on new challenges. Though it might take the spontaneity out of the practice, go ahead and pencil it into your diary. This way, you create an opportunity for you to regularly work on your mindset and EI. Additionally, by involving your child in this, you model consistency and can show them how this mindset works. You can start this practice by doing activities with your child. As they progress towards becoming more open and independent, allow them to pursue their own interests and have their own adventures.

Strategies to Build Resilience

Resilience is an extremely important quality for our children to have. This is because this quality provides them with the emotional skills and wherewithal to navigate stressful situations, overcome obstacles, and deal with failure. The persistence that comes with resilience also cultivates curiosity, creativity, and the drive to contribute more positively to the world in which your child finds themselves (Ryann, 2020).

Essential Attributes

There are many ways to teach our children how to be resilient. A lot of research has been done into this specific human attribute and how it factors into parenting. The basis for resilience has been described by Ginsburg and Moraghan Jablow (2015) as consisting of seven basic characteristics. These are the characteristics you must focus on teaching your child. If they can master these, they will be well on their way to gaining essential emotional strength. The seven basic tenets of resilience are:

- Competence

- Confidence

- Connection

- Character

- Contribution

- Coping skills

- Control

Teaching Your Child How to Overcome Obstacles

Resilience involves a great deal of emotional athleticism. More specifically, teaching our children this skill means teaching them to deal with the rocks that life will inevitably throw across their path. Below, you will find 10 easy strategies that will help imbue your child with the qualities of perseverance and consistency. Given that each of them is a teaching technique, keep your child's learning style in mind as you implement them. Consider altering them in such a way that they will resonate with your child most profoundly.

The 10 tips for teaching a child how to overcome are:

1. Never forget that you are a role model: Your children will learn how to deal with their own problems by seeing how you deal with yours. Demonstrate to your children how you approach obstacles and the reasoning behind your actions. It's essential that your kids know that you work to overcome your obstacles; otherwise, they may feel inclined to either give up or outsource this responsibility.

2. Ensure that your kids follow through: While we already know how to encourage our kids to keep on trying despite setbacks, it's also important that we teach them the skill of consequence. If your child can solve a problem on their own, let them do so. With enough practice, they will find themselves doing this of their own accord.

3. Know when you have to step in: Encouraging our children in the face of adversity is one thing but supporting them to continue a futile endeavor is quite another. If you see that they are struggling too much or that the path they are walking will lead to a dead end, it's your parental obligation to step in. Once again, don't take over completely. Rather, share your thoughts with them, and help them brainstorm alternate routes to take or backup plans if the first one doesn't pan out. When it comes to implementation, you have to return to your role as a supportive spectator.

4. Don't send them out into the world with a half-empty emotional tool belt: Resilience is an excellent skill and quality to have. It is also one that is made up of other skills and qualities linked to EI. Teach and model the components of resilience, namely self-confidence, perseverance, motivation, faith, good judgment, strength of character, and basic problem-solving skills (All Pro Dad, 2010).

5. Get the whole family involved and make problem-solving a game: This can be anything from doing puzzles together to going on scavenger hunts or attempting an escape room. The activity itself isn't all that important. However, it must demonstrate to your child that problems are a part of life and that solving them supplements and enriches their lived experience. When selecting an activity, make sure that it will require your child to use and build their problem-solving and critical-thinking skills.

6. Have open discussions as a family unit: Whenever one of you is presented with an obstacle, use the opportunity of something like a family dinner to present the issue to the household so that they can help brainstorm solutions. Crucially, you should only provide your child with ideas and opinions. Avoid dictating what their approach should be or shooting down ideas you don't agree with. They will learn by doing, and sometimes this involves rethinking their own ideas.

7. Distinguish between appropriate and inappropriate expectations: This is more for you as the parent and involves setting limits on the things you expect of your child. Expecting too much will lead to issues down the line, while expecting too little may likely cause your child to contribute to problems as opposed to

solutions. You have to find a middle way in which you task them with reasonable expectations and responsibilities without overburdening or underestimating them. Keep in mind that while they are an essential part of your household, they are still just kids.

8. Get your kids involved in charity: Sign up for some outreach programs or community drives. Look for those that will require creative and critical thinking. By helping your child solve others' problems, they gain the skills they need to overcome their own.

9. Remember to make your children well-rounded: An essential part of resilience is knowing when to shoulder the burden alone and when to ask for a helping hand. Make sure that your child learns this aspect of EI, as it will help them in life. Teach them that, as long as they know they've tried; there is no shame in asking for help. Sometimes, the very best solutions are born out of collaboration, and they may just prevent your child from feeling overwhelmed. By teaching them about both sides of the resilience coin, your kids will know when something is out of their league. When they do ask for help, they won't feel bad, and they will have avoided catastrophe.

10. Remember that practice makes perfect: Finally, remember that neither resilience nor a complete growth mindset can be developed overnight. Help your child develop these skills and attributes by giving them the chance to solve their own problems more than once or to weigh in on issues in your life. Tackle obstacles together, brainstorm solutions, and praise your child for their efforts and the results they achieve. Given enough repetition, as well as the staggered development of their abilities, your child will be as resilient as can be.

A Four-Week Guide to Introducing Your Child to the Growth Mindset

Teaching your child how to adopt an entirely new perspective on the world is a monumental task. Knowing where to begin with all the different strategies, exercises, and activities can prove overwhelming. Luckily, there's a four-week framework you can follow to help introduce the growth mindset into your child's life. This framework takes a staggered approach, teaching things gradually so as not to throw anyone in at the deep end. As with most of what we've covered in this chapter, remember that your child may not always be suited to certain approaches or methods. If you find that this is the case with the framework, take its basic components and customize them to fit your child better.

Week One: The Fundamentals

Start by sitting your child down and explaining what a mindset is. Once they grasp this, they move on to the fixed and growth variants and how they differ from one another. Make sure you cover all the different components that go into adopting a new mindset. Ensure that you discuss the science behind this process, including the concept of neuroplasticity, as well as how we have the ability to grow, change, and develop throughout our entire lives. Remember that you are introducing something entirely new to your child and that you are setting them up for the successful adoption of an array of new behavioral practices. As such, keep things lighthearted and make the learning process fun by tailoring it to their learning style.

Some steps you can take during this first week of teaching include:

- Asking your child how they understand mindsets in general as well as in terms of being fixed or geared towards growth. Ask them how they think they could adopt a new mindset and what their understanding of its meaning is. Hear them out, and correct them only when necessary.

- Share examples from your own experience. By demonstrating that you yourself have powered through challenges and adversity, you motivate your child to do the same. They will also feel that they are able to share their struggles with you, given that you will understand what they are going through.

- Don't shy away from science. Encourage your child to ask questions about the brain's ability to change and adapt. The more thoroughly they understand what happens inside as you change your mindset, the more they will realize the extent of its benefits.

Week Two: Identification

Moving into the second week, you are starting to apply that foundational knowledge practically. Along with your child, take a moment to do some introspection and identify your own mindset. Take a look around you as well, and notice the signs of fixed or growth mindsets as they present themselves to different people. If you would like to practice this observation on familiar faces, take your child's favorite film, video, or show and see if you can spot the characters' mindsets.

Similar to the first week, there are certain steps you can take to facilitate this identification:

- Reflect on the way you and your child understand the definitions of different types of mindsets. Now that you know what they are, see if you can identify a time in your life when you inhabited either or both of these mindsets.

- Practice making a positive switch. You can use the emotional transition exercise discussed earlier in this chapter to determine how you can identify the negative things you think and say about yourself. Using the rules of this exercise, help your child change their self-talk and self-awareness for the better so that they may have a more positive idea of themselves as well as of the world around them.

- Think of the process of shifting mindsets as similar to learning a new language. When you are building your vocabulary for a new language, it helps to keep some visual aids around the house, pasted to items, so that you can be reminded of the equivalent in the new language. You can do the same with a growth mindset. You don't have to put notes on your microwave, but you can create a poster or collage displaying your new emotional vocabulary. When you or your child get something wrong, refer back to your visual aid to correct yourself.

- Discuss the changes a growth mindset brings to your sensory experiences. Set time aside to talk openly with your child about all the differences in sight, sound, and feeling they notice once they begin opening their minds.

Week Three: Walk the Talk

Let your child see how you take the theory behind a growth mindset and put it into practice. This is essential if you'd like to teach your child to adopt this perspective. To make it easier for them, ensure that they see your actions in the context of everyday life. That way, they will already know which situations require which behavioral and emotional adaptations.

As you model this mindset, keep in mind that your child has to see how difficult this process may be. Remember that to falter is human, something your child should know. To help them see how the process looks practically, consider the following activities for week number three:

- Share your own past experiences with adversity, obstacles, and failure. Be honest with your child about the setbacks you have experienced in life. Walk them through how you approached and ultimately solved your problems. Remind them that you still encounter difficulties sometimes and that you are always working to sharpen your problem-solving skills. In doing so, they know they aren't alone in this.

- Extol the virtues of perseverance, and be sure to emphasize the emotional payoff of resilience and a growth mindset. Share with your child how good it felt when you allowed yourself space for growth, forgave your failures, and saw your goals through to the end. Make mention of how you gained feelings like contentment, satisfaction, and pride, as well as the boost in self-esteem that came along with this.

- Sit down with your child and set a new goal. Discuss what each of you would like to achieve in the short-term, whether this be an advancement at home, school, or work. Next, decide on a course of action together. Then, go do it. Regularly check in to share your progress and check on how your child is coming along. Your goal doesn't have to be something impressive; it must simply be something you follow through on to provide a behavioral example for your kids.

- Embrace the power of "yet."

Week Four: Repetition

No one achieves the growth they want overnight, nor do they hit it out of the park the first time they step up to the plate. Moreover, adopting this mindset takes effort, something that only becomes easier the more times you try. You have to include your child in this process of developmentally-oriented trial and error. Take them along for the ride, and as you grow alongside them, encourage them to continue trying. Remember to praise them for trying and motivate them to keep going. Along with this repetition and encouragement, remind them time and again that they are able to do what they set their mind to, even if it's not perfect from the very start. Make it fun for your child to learn, and give them the space to do it in their own way. Though this practice may start in week four, it will provide you with a framework for nourishing this growth mindset for the rest of your child's life.

Growth is an incredible thing. What's even more incredible is that any of us can do it; all we have to do is open the door to all the potential we hold within ourselves. Through this process of emotional and cognitive change, we will learn to adopt many new habits and may discover a great deal about our own internal lives. It's worth remembering that while our ultimate goal is to set our children up for emotional stability, happiness, and success, we ourselves can also stand to learn a thing or two. In the next part of our journey, we'll take a look at all there is to discover and how we can do just that.

Chapter 5:

The Path to Self-Awareness and Discovery

The most important conversations you'll ever have are the ones you'll have with yourself. –David Goggins

One of the core tenets of emotional intelligence is the ability to examine who you are and to gain a comprehensive, accurate, and objective picture. This is a long way of saying that a key aspect of EI is being self-aware. Possessing this quality allows your child to understand themselves better. By being self-aware, they understand what their emotions are and how they work with them. Additionally, self-awareness helps a child know where their limits are, what they are capable of, and how much change they can handle. This is an essential life skill to have and will form a key part of planning their lives as they progress into adulthood. The benefits of self-awareness are legion, and by exploring them, a person can come to understand how complex emotions truly are. More importantly, they can unpack this complexity and put the potential that lies within these feelings to good use.

What Is Self-Awareness?

Before we can tap into any of the perks mentioned above, we have to understand what it means to be self-aware. By definition, self-awareness is the quality of possessing a holistic comprehension of your personhood. What you are comprehending is the nature and extent of your emotions, thoughts, values, and skills. Additionally, your knowledge extends beyond just how these aspects of yourself influence your own life to understanding how they factor into your behavior as it influences the people and world around you (Ocampo, 2021).

The development of this awareness lays the foundation for many other aspects and skills associated with EI. In particular, these skills are often learned gradually as a child develops during the course of their life, and they set your child up for the acquisition of other important emotional and social abilities. It's important that we emphasize the power of self-awareness, as it can manifest relatively early in a child's life. The first signs of self-awareness can be observed as early as 15 months, while their integration into a child's functioning may happen at any point between this time and the age of two years. However, it's usually physical self-awareness that shows up first. Between 15 and 24 months, your child will begin to understand their presence as a physical being in the world (Gongala, 2015). This may sound odd and slightly existential, but physical self-awareness merely means that children recognize physical sensations as their own. If they see their hands, whether in front of their face or reflected back to them, they will recognize them as being their own. At this same age, your child can differentiate between sensations they stimulate and those brought into their sensory field by others.

There is a considerable gap between the age at which a child becomes physically self-aware and when this awareness evolves to become psychological. The latter manifests at approximately five years of age and is the type of self-awareness that is encapsulated by the definition at the top of this section. By the age of five, your child is cognizant of their existence on both a physical and psychological plane. From this age on, they increasingly come into contact with other people's emotions and learn how they differ from your child's own experiences. Psychological self-awareness is what is most pertinent for our purposes here, as its cultivation feeds directly into the development of EI.

As the years pass and your child becomes ever more aware of what goes on around and within them, we can see self-awareness evolve. Through this change, what it means to be practically self-aware starts to shift as well. For the remainder of this chapter, we will consider that healthy self-awareness is characterized by the following behaviors:

- Accurately identifying and examining emotions.

- Acceptance of imperfection and embracing a true, honest view of yourself.

- Identifying strengths, weaknesses, limits, and boundaries.

- Continuously working towards self-improvement and adopting a growth mindset.

The Importance of Being Self-Aware

While certain aspects of self-awareness, like being fully cognizant of your physical presence, are natural progressions of a child's cognitive development, psychological self-awareness must be nurtured and cultivated. This responsibility lies with us as parents, who must teach our children the importance of being honest with themselves and taking care of their emotional needs. Regardless of the many benefits to be drawn from self-awareness, it's essential that we teach its practice from a young age. By expanding our child's perspective beyond their own experiences, we teach them to become more receptive. This, in turn, makes it easier for them to adopt other aspects of emotional intelligence, such as empathy, self-regulation, and motivation. The earlier we start to help them develop the necessary traits of awareness, the sooner they will be able to start building their EI.

If this alone isn't motivation enough, the benefits of self-awareness are incredibly wide-ranging and supplement your child's ability to learn many different skills. These skills range from becoming more adept at emotional processing to more deftly handling social situations. The benefits of strong self-awareness include:

- The ability to identify individual emotions, whether simple or complex. This counts for your child's own feelings as well as those with whom they interact.

- Increased ability to empathize and exhibit compassion and kindness.

- Improved listening and verbal comprehension skills.

- Improved communication abilities, both verbal and nonverbal.

- The acquisition of critical thinking skills, including the ability to identify and analyze any inherent or unconscious biases and prejudices. These skills also include understanding what their cultural and personal values are and how they influence your child's behavior.

- The ability to create and foster more meaningful relationships in which your child connects deeply with others.

- Improved decision-making and leadership capabilities.

- Improved social skills. This particular benefit extends beyond everyday interactions and means that your child will be able to navigate difficult interpersonal interactions, specifically those that involve people from a variety of backgrounds.

- Increased levels of self-confidence and self-esteem.

- Accurately and honestly identifying their interests and knowing that their pursuit is worthwhile.

Encouraging Self-Reflection

One of the best ways in which any person can become more self-aware is by taking an honest, comprehensive, and objective look at themselves. This practice is known as self-reflection, and there are a myriad of things we can do to encourage our children to look inward.

The very first thing you can do to encourage your child to self-reflect is to accept them for the emotional being they are, as well as the one they will grow to be. This acceptance cannot be limited to an epiphany within your own consciousness. You have to acknowledge your child's emotions, both positive and negative. By showing your child that you see them emotionally, they will gain a better awareness of their internal state. In turn, this will lead them to look at their emotions differently and more closely.

This is merely the first step towards encouraging self-reflection. Simply helping your child realize there is something to be examined within isn't enough to get them to actively engage in the practice. To supplement your approach, try the following strategies:

- Allow and encourage your child to communicate freely. In doing so, you teach them to accept and acknowledge their own emotions, as well as to open up when they need to. By talking through their emotions, they can understand their like or dislike of something as well as the situations surrounding their feelings. They spend time with their emotions and get to know themselves better.

- Help your child attach labels to their emotional experiences. When you talk with them about their feelings and yours, help them learn what each word means and to which emotion it is attached. Be careful not to overwhelm them and dump the entire emotional vocabulary on them. As they mature, you can teach them about frustration, pride, jealousy, and the like. Start off with the basic terms "happy," "sad," and "angry." If you lay this foundation, their later expansion will be all the easier.

- Teach your child that there is no shame in asking for help. Doing so is one of the most self-aware things a person can do. It demonstrates that they know their abilities and limits, and know that they will benefit from someone else's assistance.

- Push your child to use their strengths. You know your child, and you know what they are good at. Remind them of the strengths you have observed and encourage them to use these skills as often as they can. This support will cause them to analyze their strengths themselves. Additionally, you have to teach them about their limits and the importance of knowing that you can't do everything or push yourself too far.

- Be honest with your child about the difficulties of life. Talk to them about the things they find easy and those that pose a challenge. Teach them that not everything in life will be easy and that obstacles are part of the human experience. Crucially, don't stop there. Instead, help them brainstorm strategies and actions to build on their strengths in order to overcome or sidestep life's hurdles.

- Teach skills for confidence. Support your child when they are feeling down, especially when those feelings manifest as expressions of their own ineptitude or failure. Encourage them to change tack, believe in themselves, and try again.

- Place emphasis on the bigger picture. It can be very easy to get caught up in the nitty-gritty of emotional intelligence and development. However, regardless of their successes or difficulties, remind your child that this is just one part of them. They are complex beings, and each part of their personhood should be nurtured and developed so that it can grow into all it can be.

- While you don't have to reality-check your child at every turn, ensure that discussions about failure don't fall by the wayside. Actively avoiding this creates stigma and shame. Encourage your child to acknowledge their weaknesses and to speak freely when they encounter difficulties. Normalize this for them by using yourself or people in their lives as examples.

- Allow them the space and support to pursue their passions. Remind your child of their strengths and encourage them to pursue these avenues. Even if your child is passionate about something they struggle with, don't discourage them. Motivate them to keep going. They will either overcome their struggles or learn a valuable lesson in limits and letting go.

- Teach your child to be a good friend. Ask them about their friends and their likes, dislikes, and dispositions. In doing so, you get them to open up about their relationships while also encouraging them to take notice of their friends and to make an effort in their relationships.

- Encourage exploration and experimentation. Allow your child to try new things so that they may learn where their strengths lie. Simultaneously, they will gauge the extent of their abilities. Don't steer them in any one direction. Rather, remind them that they don't have to be excellent at everything. What's important is that they cultivate and explore their own interests.

- Be an example for your child. We have revisited behavioral modeling time and again, and it is just as applicable here. Teach your child to be empathetic by doing the same in your interactions with them. Moreover, actively practice listening, problem-solving, and the recognition of your own failures and shortcomings.

It's worth noting that not everything works for every child and that some practices may require a bit more effort if you implement them once your child has matured a bit. For instance, talking openly about emotions and failure from a young age will help shape your child's mind during those first, formative years. Employing this practice after they have started schooling may be slightly more difficult, as they will have developed different ideas and will have an idea of what the world considers taboo. Regardless of the effort level, don't give up. Teaching your child self-reflection brings them one step closer to achieving self-awareness, which in turn helps them become the emotionally intelligent individual you know they can be.

Activities to Improve Self-Awareness

Now that we know what self-awareness is and how we can encourage its formulation through self-reflection, it's time to look at more practical approaches. To help our children accurately gauge who they are and who they want to become, we can undertake any number of exercises. It is important to remember that, while our goal is to improve emotional intelligence that will last a lifetime, we are teaching these skills to children. As such, try to make the activities fun. Maybe even consider adjusting them so that they suit your child's sensibilities and disposition more closely. In doing so, there's a greater chance that these lessons and skills will stick.

Positive Awareness

Using a pen and a piece of paper, have your child create a holistic picture of themselves. In order to strengthen their self-awareness and encourage them to focus on their positive attributes, have them write down a list of all the things they like about themselves. Ensure that the scope of the activity is comprehensive by helping them cover all the different aspects of their personhood. Give them prompts so that they write down all the good things about them across the emotional, physical, and cognitive realms. Once the list has been completed, put it in a place of prominence where your child will see it regularly and be reminded of all the good parts of themselves.

Emotional Check-In

This activity can be integrated into your household's daily routine. In the morning, before everyone goes their separate ways, discuss how you are feeling as well as what your expectations and intentions for the day are. In the evening, once everyone is back home, check in again to see how the day went. Ask about your child's emotional experiences, the problems they encountered, what they achieved that day, and which tasks they couldn't manage. Share the summary of your own day in turn to encourage open discussion.

The Thoughts-Actions-Feelings Circle

This exercise was first constructed by the online educational platform Positive Action (2020) and required us to lay out the chain of cognitive and emotional events that underlie human behavior. In doing so, we understand how our thoughts motivate our actions, which in turn motivate our feelings. After this, the cycle starts to repeat once more.

Help your child understand and unpack this cycle by having them write down a scenario they have recently experienced. The nature of this experience can be either positive or negative, though the latter might perhaps lead to greater self-awareness. Once they have written down the scenario, have them write down what they think about it. They can write about what jumped into their minds, the conclusions they drew, and the internal responses they had. Next, they can write down either the actions they took or the emotions they felt. Once all three have been noted, examine how one fed into the other and what your child's state of mind was at the end of the experience. Repeat this exercise when your child is presented with a difficult scenario. However, do this before they act so that they may map out their approach and understand what they truly feel.

Emotion Journal

As a long-term exercise, your child can keep a journal in which they write down each of their emotional responses to situations and interactions they experience throughout the day. For younger children, ask them to simply identify their feelings. They can do this through words or pictures. For older kids, ask them to write down the context of the emotion as well as explain how this particular emotional experience made them feel physically, socially, and mentally.

If you are unsure of how to help your child start their journaling, provide them with prompts. Though many of these are aimed at emotional exploration, the ultimate goal is self-awareness, so the scope of the journal may extend beyond feelings. Provide your child with the following prompts for guidance:

- When you were with your friends today, how did you feel?

- When you look back on today and everything you did, how does your recollection make you feel?

- When you woke up this morning, how did you feel?

- Is there a place in the world that means a lot to you? If yes, what do you feel when you are there?

- Is there anything you really love to do? What is it, and how does this activity make you feel?

- Who is your closest friend in the world? Describe their personality.

- You have an event coming up soon. How do you feel about it?

- Your parents recently handed down a punishment. Do you think it was fair, and do you think what you did warranted that punishment?

- What are you excited about in the near future?

- What are you afraid of, and do you have a way to overcome this fear?

Gratitude List

A gratitude list helps children become self-aware by taking a look at their lives and recognizing all the good things they have going for them. This exercise is easy enough, as your child simply makes a list of all the things for which they feel grateful. Discuss the list with them, and ask them if they can see how these things influence other parts of their lives. Update this list every month so your child can remain aware of each thing contributing to their happiness.

Positive Affirmations

This exercise helps children adopt a more positive outlook on life as well as speak about themselves and the things around them in a more optimistic way. Its intention is similar to the gratitude list so that they may see what they are capable of and how thoroughly happiness is present throughout their lives. You can teach your child some affirmations they can use when in distress. Alternatively, you can make the affirmations part of your daily routine to help your child integrate this positivity into their regular functioning.

Though you can customize the affirmations you use, you can also use the following as a framework:

- I can do whatever I set my mind to.

- I am not afraid of failure and will learn from the times that I do not succeed.

- The way I feel about myself comes from within, not from the words of others.

- I feel proud of what I have accomplished.

- I am smart and can open my mind to learning new skills.

- I am creative and can create good solutions to my problems.

- I am worthy of love and support.

- I don't have to change who I am or the things I like just to make others happy.

- I deserve to be happy and to take pride in who I am.

- I will do my best, and that will be good enough.

Goals

Help your child set goals aimed at improving their self-awareness. When they achieve these goals, they learn more about themselves and their strengths. If they fail, they still gain some self-awareness as they learn about their limits and problem-solving skills. We will be covering goals more in-depth later in this chapter. For now, all we need to know is that goals help our kids gain experience with motivation and provide them with the opportunity to explore their abilities.

Use Strengths

Help your child identify their strengths. With these in mind, brainstorm activities and pursuits that will help your child build on these same strengths. Not only does this help them gain a stronger, more positive self-image, but it also helps them learn new skills and build upon those they already have. Along the way, your child will learn where some of their strengths stop and how much potential lies in others. As they undertake the activities meant to build these aspects of their abilities, support them, and allow them to explore on their own.

Self-Compliments

You can help build your child's self-esteem and self-worth by praising them. However, no words will be more impactful than those they speak to themselves. Your child can write these compliments down as a list or in a journal. Be sure to keep these words close by so that your child may revisit these positive things in times of distress. Some self-compliments your child can use include:

- I am strong because…

- Who I am now is good, and I am a good person.

- I am good at doing…

- I make the people around me smile and laugh, and I contribute to their happiness.

- I am beautiful, smart, and capable.

- What I have done today is good, and it is worth sharing with other people.

- I have good friends, and I am a good friend to them.

- I feel excited for the time ahead, and that is something I can enjoy.

- I love my family, and I deserve the love they give me.

- I did that all by myself! I should be proud of what I achieved.

Uncovering and Nurturing Your Child's Hidden Talents

Your child becomes more self-aware the more they understand their strengths and weaknesses. Allowing your child to discover and explore their talents is part of this. Along the way, trial and error, missteps, and perseverance will all form part of your child's emotional vocabulary. By the end of the process, they will have discovered their niche and can focus on carving out that particular spot in the world for themselves.

Knowing how to discover and handle your child's talents can be a tricky business. So, employ the following steps to make sure they find what they love and that they get better at doing it.

Observe Your Child

When we looked at learning styles, we saw the benefits of taking a step back and simply watching your child exist in space. This practice is similar to that. Take note of your kid's actions and words throughout the day as they move from one space to another. Watch out for things towards which they gravitate, as well as how they respond to tasks or situations handed to them and which they have no choice but to see through. Make a list of the natural talents, proclivities, and preferences you see in your child. To gain a comprehensive picture, consider speaking to their teachers and caregivers, who will be able to tell you how your child behaves when they are not under your watchful eye.

Get Your Child to Weigh In

Ask them outright what they would like to do and which activities or skills they would like to pursue. As you do so, remember to keep an open mind. Your child wasn't made using the "Copy+Paste" function. They are individualized people who have their own likes, dislikes, skills, and preferences. Hear them out and, if it is feasible, enable them to pursue the expansion of their talents. Remember to continue supporting them all the way.

Allow Them to Explore New Things

Naturally, your child has to find the things to which they are best suited, and in order to do this, they will need some room to explore. If your child is young or if they are wading into unfamiliar waters, allowing this exploration can be very worrying for you as a parent. It's important to note that just because you are allowing them to go out and experiment, this does not mean that you are giving them free rein. You can provide them with new options in a safe environment under your supervision. Listen to your child when they tell you what they want to explore. Allow them time and space to pick something up, try it, and decide whether they would like to continue with it.

Praise Over Proclivity

Some children are naturally good at certain things. However, most will have to build their skills and knowledge over time. It's important that we don't focus too much on these natural talents, as they lie beyond our children's control. Instead, focus on the effort they put in and the work they do to excel at their talents. In doing so, you teach them about perseverance, motivation, and having confidence in what they can do. Encouraging your child's efforts as opposed to their natural-born ability also helps them on their way to adopting a growth mindset.

Encourage Learning Through Recreation

Eventually, your child will learn to put their own spin on the particulars of their talents. When they are first starting out, however, the best way for them to pick up new skills is by observing and mimicking other people's methods. Expose your child to the techniques and actions of people who have excelled in the field related to their talent. Crucially, make it clear to your child that mimicry is simply a way for them to gain a fundamental understanding of how they can practice their talent. Ensure that they know that they will eventually have to adopt their own specific approach and tailor their techniques to be more personalized.

Use Books and Films as Learning Aids

Using these media to help your child gain a basic grasp of new activities will make things more accessible and will help them understand their interests in a way that they can relate to. Choose age-appropriate content that demonstrates the ins and outs of a particular activity in a fun and relatable way. If your child's interest is piqued after the first attempt, introduce them to more pieces and see if their passion sticks.

Make Art Supplies Accessible

Keep paints, crayons, clay, and colored paper at the ready. You can construct a kit with all of these items to make them more portable. Oftentimes, your child will want to express their passion for an activity through something creative. Sometimes, creativity is the activity that they most like to engage in. If you combine these types of crafts with some of your child's other activities, their brains will be all the more engaged, and the learning process will be all the more impactful.

Venture Into the Great Outdoors

In the bright, open spaces of nature, your child will have boundless opportunities to explore the world around them. They become aware of natural processes, the seasons, and the beauty of nature. In addition to the exploration that might steer them in the direction of the sciences, they can also run around, play games, and try out some sports. Taking your children outside regularly provides them with all the space they need to experiment and unlock a hidden talent. Worse comes to worse, and they find they hate the outdoors. At least they will know their passions lie somewhere outside of, well, the outside.

Incorporate Music Into Everyday Life

Another method of creative expression is through music. Play music for your children whenever you can to encourage them to find the style of music that appeals to them most. If you find that they have a desire to make their own music, provide them with some instruments as well as the opportunity to engage with the music they like. Even if they have no desire to make music, encourage your child to use listening, singing, or dancing to music as a means of expression and a sort of emotional outlet.

Immerse Them in Culture

Take your children to museums, zoos, galleries, aquariums, and the theater to expose them to many different aspects of cultures as well as different disciplines they can study and pursue. The more they see, the better they will be able to suss out what it is that truly interests them and nurture those talents. Even if your child doesn't find something they love on these outings, it's still time spent together.

Find and Pursue Your Own Desires and Talents

Finally, we return to the notion of behavioral modeling. Children may be afraid to pursue things that interest them. Perhaps they are afraid of failure or of the hard work it will require. Perhaps they think it's not worth doing as just a hobby. It's up to you to demonstrate to your child how fulfilling it is to pursue the things that you are good at and that make you happy. Ensure that they see you overcoming obstacles and fear. Remember that you are their first point of reference when growing up. If you show them you can do it, they will believe they can, too.

Goal-Setting

The purpose of this chapter is to help us encourage our children to explore the world around them, as well as the one within them that's populated with their thoughts, emotions, behaviors, and beliefs. Part of helping them understand this world is helping them achieve their desires and aspirations. This, in turn, is made possible through goal-setting. Within the context of child-rearing, Li (2022a) defines goal-setting "as committing to achieve a target result in an activity." Additionally, this practice is regarded as one of the most effective ways to teach your child the attribute of motivation as well as the importance of dedication.

The term "goal-setting" refers to the construction of objectives of any kind. Under this umbrella term, we find a variety of different types. More specifically, there are seven different types of goals that we can achieve through the process of goal-setting. Canfield (2007) has identified these types as follows:

1. Career goals.

2. Financial goals.

3. Personal goals, also known as goals for personal development.

4. Spiritual goals.

5. Educational or academic goals.

6. Relationship goals.

7. Physical and health goals.

None of these types are more important than the others. However, at certain points in life, some may take a higher priority than others. For instance, as a child, educational and personal goals may be of greater importance than relationship, financial, or career goals. Regardless of the nature of your objective, there are a number of benefits to be gained from the practice of goal-setting. Through setting goals, children are able to catalyze and take control of their personal development. Moreover, by physically constructing a plan to reach their objectives, they learn one of the core tenets of emotional intelligence: motivation (Connors, 2019).

In addition to this, goal-setting enables children to focus on their aspirations as well as build up their confidence in their learning and practical abilities. By setting and subsequently achieving a goal, children get a boost in their self-esteem. Even if they fail to achieve their desired result, they will still feel this improvement, largely through their demonstration of dedication and perseverance. By giving children the responsibility of constructing and pursuing a goal, we teach them how to be accountable for their actions and the solutions they brainstorm. If we start early, we can imbue our children with these qualities as they develop. As our children grow and change, these skills will do the same.

Setting SMART Goals

Chances are you have encountered the concept of a SMART goal before. This acronym is a valuable tool. It acts as a framework according to which we can structure our goals and devise a plan to reach them to the best of our abilities. Constructing a goal involves using each of the acronym's letters, which are detailed as follows:

- Specific: Make your goals as specific as possible. Vague or broad objectives will complicate their achievement. The more specific your child is, the more detailed the plan for its attainment can be, which increases the probability of success. When determining the specificity of a goal, you can use the five W's—who, what, when, where, and why.

- Measurable: There has to be a way for your child to quantify their success in achieving their goal. If your child doesn't have an end point they want to reach, they will continue to work into perpetuity without ever feeling that sense of fulfillment that comes with reaching an objective. This ties in with the specificity of the goal. Have some sort of metric to use when your child hits their goal. You can even use this to track milestones along the way. For instance, don't simply set a goal to make more friends. Instead, set a goal to make five new friends.

- Achievable: It's natural to dream big, and ambition is never a bad quality for a child to possess. However, when it comes to setting goals, it may be advisable for them to aim for something closer to home than the stars. Whatever they hope to achieve should be within reach, either by using the skills they already possess or by building on these skills while learning a few new ones. An easy way to tick this letter off is to take one of your child's large goals and break it down into smaller parts. These will be more achievable, and the achievement of each one will bring your child closer to their bigger objective.

- Relevant: It's essential that your child doesn't set random goals. Ensure that the things they hope to achieve are linked to the areas of life in which they need to improve. While constructing their goals, children must keep in mind what their strengths and weaknesses are and work towards improving on both. Alternatively, when setting goals for EI, try to construct something that will help them acquire skills connected to one of the five core tenets.

- Time-Bound: In the same way that our kids must know when they have achieved their goals, they have to put a cap on the timeline of their pursuit. Choosing a deadline and sticking to it will help to motivate your child and ensure that they see the process all the way through.

So, how do we go about setting SMART goals? If we understand the meaning behind the acronym, we and our children can start building our goals so that we are one step closer to a state of elevated EI. Keeping the SMART formula in mind, our goal-setting can be done in five easy steps. They are:

1. Identifying the goal: Have your child figure out what it is they hope to achieve. The more genuine their desire for the end result, the more dedicated they will be to seeing the goal through. Remind your child that they will be the ones pursuing the goal, and as such, it should truly matter. Ask them what they hope to achieve, either immediately or down the line. If they get stuck, give them some examples of goals from your own life. However, don't give them the answer, but guide them towards their own realization.

2. Determining the purpose of the goal: For this step, your child has to be able to answer the question, "Why?" They have to be able to tell you why they are hoping to achieve this particular objective. More than simply helping nail down the specifics of their goal, knowing the purpose will help keep your child motivated. If they know what they want and why they want it, they can keep this end result in mind when they get discouraged.

3. Establish a timeline: Determine whether this goal will be achieved in the short-term, in the long term, or whether your child hopes to reach their objective in the immediate future. Based on the particulars of the goal, make sure that it is reasonable and realistic. Consider your child's age and their abilities. For children between

three and five, consider goals with a timeline no longer than a day. As children mature, extend the deadline to a week or a month after the initial goal-setting process (Kristenson, 2022).

4. Construct a plan of action: Using a worksheet or a template, break up the pursuit of your child's goal into smaller, manageable steps. Make sure that each step is within your child's abilities or that those who require new skills follow steps in which these skills are learned. Make sure that the plan is written down. This will help your child stay on track and hold them accountable for their actions as they work towards their objective.

5. Track, support, and celebrate: Once the goal and the plan have been put into place, it is time for your child to assume responsibility for their achievement. Keep their plan in a prominent place where they will be reminded of it. Make sure that they keep track of their own progress and that they tick off each step they complete. When they encounter difficulties, support, and encourage them without taking the problem off their hands. When they hit a milestone, complete a step, or achieve their desired end result, don't forget to celebrate your child and recognize their accomplishments.

Tips for Setting Goals

Now that you know how the process works, you can fine-tune your approach to goal-setting, particularly when it comes to helping your children. When they are starting the process of setting goals, help them set effective goals by using some tips. Start by letting your child decide and set their own goals. Having your children determine what it is they wish to pursue will not only make the goal more personal but will also make them more dedicated to its achievement.

The process of achieving goals isn't instantaneously mastered. It takes time to gain the skills and attributes to see these things through. As such, start with smaller, short-term goals and build up from there. Examples of easily-implemented goals include:

- Save enough money to buy a new toy before the start of the summer.

- Read one book a month that isn't part of schoolwork.

- Practice drawing for 30 minutes every day for two weeks.

- Work on building that Lego set for an hour every day until it is completed.

- Make a new friend on the first day of school.

Break up the goals into smaller, manageable chunks. This will prevent your child from getting discouraged and will help them see the process all the way through.

Avoid the pitfalls that are commonly linked to the goal-setting process. First and foremost, don't let your child overburden themselves with too many goals at once. Start off with one or two and allow them to set up more as they expand their skills and knowledge. By beginning small, they will learn about their skills of perseverance. Secondly, don't stray from the SMART system. Life is unpredictable, and external forces or events may intervene and try to distract your child from their goal. Stick to the SMART system so that they may see their goals through to the end, even if they don't entirely succeed.

For the purposes of adhering to this system, ask your child some SMART goal-setting questions. These questions will help them determine what they truly want and how they will achieve it. Use each letter of the acronym as a framework for these questions. The following are examples of questions you can ask:

- **S**: Is the goal specific? What is the desired end result? How will it influence or change your life? What do you hope will happen once you have reached your goal?

- **M**: Is the goal measurable? What metric will you use to determine your progress? Will you track your progress using milestones, or will you only measure it upon completion? What will your goal look like?

- **A**: Is the goal achievable? Which skills do you need to reach your goal? Do you have all these skills, and what will you do to learn those you don't possess? Which obstacles do you think you might encounter? How will you deal with any difficulties that come your way?

- **R**: Is the goal relevant? Why exactly do you want to achieve this particular goal? Will this goal improve your life in any way? Based on where you are now in your life, will this goal help you get to where you want to be? How can this goal help prepare you for the next chapter?

- **T**: Is the goal time-bound? By what date do you expect to finish this goal? How much time per day will you commit to this goal? If you don't reach your goal by the intended deadline, could you postpone its achievement?

We conclude this section on goal-setting tips by looking at some sample goals. The goals outlined below are all constructed using the SMART system and can serve as inspiration for your child. Take note of the voice in which the goals are written and help your child model their own accordingly.

1. I will have read two entire books by the end of this month. Both books will be fiction and will be no shorter than 200 pages. I will read at least two chapters each night and start the second book the day after I finish the first. By reading these books, I will be able to improve my reading and comprehension skills. I will also expand my vocabulary. These books will give me something to talk about in class and with my friends. No more than two weeks will be dedicated to each book. If I go over this, I will give myself a month and a half.

2. I will paint a picture of my immediate family. The picture will include myself, my mom, my dad, and my sister. Every day, I will spend two hours working on the drawing, sketching, and coloring of at least one person. I hope to do this because it will improve my artistic skills. I can practice drawing because I love art and want to get better at it. The first version of my picture will be done within two weeks, and the whole thing will be finished by the end of the month.

Goal-Setting Activities

Remember that you are teaching goal-setting to children, who learn best when they are engaged and when the people around them also participate in the learning process. Make goals fun by having you and your child perform any of the following activities:

- Creating a family bucket list: Get the whole household involved and compile a list of all the goals you each hope to achieve. Make this a group activity by writing down all the goals that the family wants to achieve. Set a reasonable timeline. Consider that this involves all of you, so give the goals a few months. At the end of the timeline, gather the family again to review what you have achieved. Discuss your experiences, what you learned, what you would do differently, and the new goals you have in mind for the household.

- Construct a wheel of fortune: This exercise helps you demonstrate to your kids how goals can be set for each of life's areas. Draw a circle and divide it into six segments, namely Home, School, Family, Friends, Hobbies, and Skills. In each segment, ask your child to construct a SMART goal.

- Make a vision board: This activity will help your child lay out the entirety of their goal in front of them. Create it by cutting out pictures that represent your desired end result. Create a collage with these pictures, buzz words, motivational phrases, and any other decor related to the goal. Working from one end to another, ask your child to walk you through each item's meaning and its relation to their objective. For an added level of accountability, have them write each explanation down.

- Play "Three Stars and A Wish:" This game can involve the entire family, or you can play it one-on-one with your child. Start by conceptualizing three separate stars, each one representing a strength or activity in which your child excels. Next, set a goal in the form of a wish. Make sure the wish is linked to all three stars and that it focuses on the improvement of these skills. The wish can be an area in which they'd like to improve or something they simply think needs work.

- Draw an interest map: This activity requires more complex cognitive skills and may not be suited to young children. Start by asking your child to write down all of their interests, favorite things, and activities they enjoy. Work with your child to examine each item on their list to determine whether there is a pattern among them. Next, draw the map by drawing circles and grouping similar items close to one another. Finally, tackle each group of circles on the map individually by setting goals that focus on the development of each one. Take each section one by one until your child has reached a goal for each of the good things in their life.

- Construct a goal ladder: Also known as "stair-step goals," this exercise helps you and your child break down their goals into smaller, more achievable steps. You can perform this activity on a piece of lined paper, or you can draw a ladder or some steps to use as a template. At the top, have your child write their ideal dream. At the bottom, have them write their first goal using the SMART system. Then, have them write their second and third goals on the next rungs of the ladder. Continue constructing these goals until they reach the dream. Help your child find the ladder more appealing by decorating it in a similar way to the vision board with motivational drawings and decorations.

Setting goals is not always an easy thing to do. Luckily, there are a large number of different strategies, exercises, and methods you can employ to help your child put together their goals and achieve everything they could hope for. By knowing what they want and what they will do to attain it, your child engages in self-reflection to determine what is missing from their life or what needs improvement. It may seem like a circuitous route, but it all eventually leads back to improving their self-awareness. Once they understand the nature of their personhood, they can move on to learning how to manage its more unruly aspects. As we move into the next chapter, it's worth remembering that as our children get bigger, their emotions grow right along with them. And though this may bring with it a few bumps in the road, knowing how to deal with these types of emotions is an essential component of a healthy EI.

Chapter 6:

Embracing Big Feelings

Our feelings are not there to be cast out or conquered. They're there to be engaged and expressed with imagination and intelligence. –T.K. Coleman

As we help our children along the road to building strong emotional intelligence, they will pick up a number of skills along the way. In addition to gaining prowess in practices such as self-reflection and emotional comprehension, an essential component of teaching our kids to use their EI is enabling them to extend this comprehension to more difficult emotional experiences. However, along with this understanding, our children also need to know how to deal with and work through these experiences. This practice, known as emotional regulation, will enable our children to understand what they are feeling, why they are feeling it, and why it is an important part of their lived experience.

Understanding Your Child's Emotions

In the previous chapter, we explored the link between our thoughts and emotions and how one feeds into the other, creating that internal cycle known as the human experience. Sometimes, we may find ourselves perplexed by our children's actions and the behavioral patterns they keep perpetuating. However, just because we are confused now doesn't mean we have to stay confused forever. There are a variety of different approaches we can employ in order to understand what your child is feeling. These approaches become part of our parenting repertoire and may not only help us to delve deeper into our children's internal state but may also enlighten us about certain aspects of our own personhood in the process.

Mentalizing

Mentalizing is an established practice within the science of psychology. In this context, the American Psychiatric Association (n.d.) defines this practice as "the ability to understand one's own and others' mental states, thereby comprehending one's own and others' intentions and affects." This generalized version of the concept is applied to parenting, the treatment of borderline personality disorder, and the attachment style that forms between a parent and their child. Additionally, mentalization-based treatment (MBT) has emerged as a legitimate form of psychotherapy used to treat mental health disorders.

For our purposes here, we must examine the practice within the context of child-rearing. When tied to parenting, mentalizing refers to our capacity to understand the mental states, emotions, thoughts, and needs that underlie and inform our children's behaviors. Because of the link between our own actions and those of our kids, parental mentalizing expands to apply this same awareness and comprehension to our behaviors and their impact upon our children's lives (Borelli & Lai, 2019). This practice has incredible and powerful potential, as it helps us to delve deeper into our children's emotions and explore the causes and factors that lie beneath the surface. In doing so, we can get to the root of their behaviors, thoughts, and feelings. If we manage to do this, we are able to help our children understand the true nature of their inner lives, which in turn will give them greater control over their life's events.

On face value alone, implementing mentalizing into your parental practice may seem daunting. However, in the spirit of the concept, if you look a little bit further, you will see that you can start to employ parental mentalizing tactics today. All you have to do is follow four easy steps:

1. Engage in emotional self-reflection. When you first start using mentalizing, you may find this practice most effective in times of emotional distress. However, you can self-reflect at any time and examine your thoughts and feelings, as well as their impact on your child. Over time, cultivate the habit of checking in with yourself. Pay regular attention to your internal experiences, and do so objectively. Gaining this perspective on your thoughts and feelings will help you deal with them, as well as lend a hand in managing your child's experiences.

2. Take a step back to reflect on your child's internal state. Whether their behavior is positive or negative, make a point of examining what they are doing and what may lead to their actions. Try to suss out what they are feeling and thinking, and which desires or needs they are communicating through their behavior. As you undertake this analysis, remember that human emotions are complex and nuanced. Your child may be feeling a particular emotion, but their behavior may reflect another entirely. This is because they don't yet possess the vocabulary to accurately express what's going on inside.

3. Be engaging. Don't just draw conclusions about what your child is experiencing; ask them about what's going on with them. Express your curiosity by asking your child some questions about their life and their experiences. Make sure to keep your questions open-ended to avoid steering your child toward any specific

answers or details. By asking these questions, you give your child a nudging prompt that will allow them to speak freely and openly.

4.   Keep an open mind. Create an environment in which your child feels safe and secure enough to share their experiences with you. However, regardless of how much they have shared or what you have observed, don't make the mistake of assuming you know your kids inside and out. Chances are, you have a good idea, but keep asking them about their experiences. Remember that your children are constantly developing and changing, and so the intricacies of their emotional state may change along with them. Your child may grow to have new reactions to the same situations. Don't dismiss these new perspectives; use them to help both of you understand the emotions tied to them.

Tips to Understand Your Child's Emotional Experiences

Even with the practice of parental mentalizing firmly attached to our child-rearing tool belts, it can still be difficult to gauge what's going on inside your child's head. To gain a clearer perspective on your child's emotional life, there are some helpful, constructive habits you can adopt.

The Power of Observation

You can never go wrong by paying attention to what your child is doing. Observe your child as they move through life and take an interest in what they say, do, express, and present themselves as. Crucially, your observation must be passive and free of judgment. Take this opportunity to learn more about your child as an individual, as opposed to how they measure up to you, their siblings, or their friends. Use this to simply become aware of who your child is. In doing so, you will learn about their uniqueness and gain insight into who they truly are and how they function.

Make Time for Quality Time

There is very little you will learn about your child from a distance. Though you can go out and do something together, quality time can be something as simple as sitting down and having a conversation. Alternatively, you can simply exist in the same space. This will still be significant and may also help you with your observation. If you opt for the former, ask them about their friends, interests, favorite things, how school is going, and what makes them happy. Make a concerted effort to get to know your child well.

Give Your Undivided Attention

As parents, our minds dart from one thing to another constantly. In doing this, we miss a lot. Set some time aside to focus your entire awareness on your child and turn your consciousness to the moment in which you find yourself. Though you can just be in one another's company, they will feel that you are paying attention if you participate in activities together. Do something that appeals to your child and that you know they will enjoy. Ensure that it is something that will require your full attention so that your mind or behavior doesn't wander. This will make your child feel special and will help strengthen your bond.

Consider Their Environment

Your child doesn't exist in a vacuum. Their beliefs, behaviors, and attitudes are influenced by the world around them. Make an effort to analyze the environments in which your child exists and to determine whether their influence is positive or negative. Help create an environment that is conducive to emotional safety and expression.

Understand the Science

The role of the parent in the development of a child's psyche is so potent that they are sometimes referred to as "neuro architects" (Gold, 2014). Given how influential you are, it may be helpful to understand how you impact the development of your child's brain and disposition. What you do helps to shape your child's brain and has an impact on neuroplasticity, a concept we have already encountered.

It is said that positive interactions and behaviors will help stimulate the brain towards positive, healthy growth. Conversely, harsh, or distressing circumstances and interactions will negatively influence the brain's development. Through this understanding, you can avoid overt negativity and harshness, opting instead to employ more positive parenting techniques to help your child's mind reach its full potential.

Acknowledge Different Methods of Expression

Some kids will feel best understood through speaking, while others will want to draw or write as a means of expressing and understanding themselves. Others will still want to engage in some sort of activity to help them communicate their thoughts and feelings. Whatever your child's chosen method, support them and allow them the space to utilize the technique that suits them. If they choose to share with you what they hope to express, try not to overanalyze what they present to you. Even when prompted to do so, keep an open mind, and accept it when your child corrects you with regards to what they hoped to convey.

Understand and Consider Your Child's Temperament

Your child's temperament is specific to them and encompasses those traits that inform their perspective on the world, their actions, and the way in which they approach interpersonal interactions. A person's temperament is shaped through experience to an extent, but this is largely an inherent part of an individual's personhood (Moravcik Walbert, 2021).

A person's temperament is a complicated, multifaceted thing. The American Academy of Pediatrics (2019) has identified nine core characteristics that constitute a temperament. Your child may not exhibit all nine but instead have a disposition made up of a specific combination of them. These characteristics are:

- Activity level refers to how much physical activity your child exhibits in their daily life. This includes physical activity, movement, restlessness, and general mobility.

- Rhythmicity or regularity, which describes the absence or presence of patterns in your child's life. These patterns apply to natural physical functions such as sleep, digestive habits, and appetite.

- Approach and withdrawal describe the way in which your child responds to the introduction of a new stimulus. These stimuli can range from new people, new places, or even changes in routine.

- Adaptability is a quality that demonstrates how well your child changes tack or adjusts to new situations, experiences, and all the changes they bring along with them.

- Intensity, more specifically, as it is linked to energy levels. This energy is tied to your child's situational responses, both positive and negative.

- Mood, as it manifests in your child's behaviors and verbalizations. This mood is said to encompass your child's friendliness, pleasantness, and general emotional disposition, whether good or bad.

- Attention span, which denotes your child's ability to focus on and conclude a task without deviating from their action plan or giving into distractions.

- Distractibility, which measures your child's resolve against the diversion of their attention by environmental stimuli.

- Sensory threshold, which describes how much stimulation your child requires in order to elicit a response of some kind. For some children, this threshold is incredibly low, while others will require a great quantity of stimuli in order to get going.

It is essential that you take your child's temperament into account when trying to discover the complexities of their emotional life. As with most other techniques in this book, you have to start with yourself. Consider your own temperament and how it comes into play during interactions with your child. Consider the fact that because temperaments tend to be divergent, your disposition may clash slightly with that of your child. Despite these differences, it's important to acknowledge your child's temperament so that you can see their positive attributes more easily. Keep your influence in mind, and know that this acknowledgment on your part may lead your children to see these good parts of themselves as well.

The best way to support your children's temperament, beyond acknowledgment, is acceptance. Just because you and your child may differ in certain aspects doesn't mean that they need to be changed. You can teach them to hone their EI without attempting to make their temperament more akin to yours. Accept your child for who they are and work on supporting them from where they are, emotionally speaking. In doing so, you will learn more about their personalities and teach them the importance of individuality.

Help Your Child Identify and Express Their Emotions

If we hope to have our children come to terms with the complex landscape of feelings that lives inside them, we have to begin by helping them identify its different components. In addition to this, we must equip them with the skills and wherewithal to take these components and communicate them to the world effectively. For us as parents, this involves two main practices: labeling and encouraging.

Naming Emotions

As we know by now, emotions are pretty much present in a person's mind from the moment they enter this world. However, despite the innate nature of emotions, learning these feelings are and how to describe them is something of a learning curve. It is with that in mind that we must take it upon ourselves to teach our children how to build up an emotional vocabulary. For young kids, especially, the best way for them to understand what they are feeling is for us to take note of their emotions and assign the correct label (Goh, 2017).

Over time, your child's young and malleable mind will learn to associate the words you teach them with the sensations they experience inside. If all goes well, they will learn to make these designations themselves as they grow older. This doesn't mean that they understand emotions entirely, but at the very least, it provides them with a foundational comprehension of what it means to feel and what these feelings are.

In general, we see young children express six main emotions, namely:

- Happiness

- Sadness

- Anger

- Fear

- Disgust

- Surprise

Your child will demonstrate these six emotions at their most basic levels when they are young. However, as your children mature and gain a more nuanced understanding of emotions, they may start to combine these feelings or experience them at more profound levels. Happiness may expand to include amusement, excitement, and euphoria. Sadness may transition into moroseness or depression. The remaining four will also evolve and become more complex the older your child becomes.

In order to prepare our children for the evolution of their emotions, we can employ a number of tools. The first, and perhaps most accessible, of these, is the feeling wheel. True to its name, a feelings wheel is a circular diagram on which emotional labels are laid out. Ordinarily, the six most basic emotions children feel will be arranged at the very center of the wheel. As you move further outward towards the edge of the circle, these feelings become more complicated, gaining new layers and attributes. As your child gets older, you can help them identify their feelings by using the different layers.

Many examples of feeling wheels can be found online, most of which will be color-coded according to the specific emotion. This tool is mainly used for children who have undergone some sort of trauma so that they may have help describing how it has affected them. However, it is still exceptionally effective for children who have had no such experiences. These wheels help your child expand their emotional vocabulary. If something bad happens to them or they encounter adversity, the knowledge they gain from the wheel will help them label and communicate their emotions.

Encourage Naming and Expressing

The second part of understanding our children, encouragement, is intended to teach our children how natural both the experience and the expression of emotions are. In order to facilitate this understanding on both sides, let's take a look at some strategies you can employ to help your child along.

Start With Words

Once more, the onus falls on you as the parent to show your kids what to do and how to do it. Get the conversation rolling by sharing your own emotional experiences with your children, as well as the ways in which you express these feelings healthily. Talk them through a number of scenarios you have encountered in your life. Once you have done this, have them demonstrate their understanding by presenting them with a hypothetical situation. Have them describe what they would do in response, then help them evaluate whether their reaction was appropriate and learn what they could do to improve.

Connect With Your Kids

This is especially essential for young kids, as they require a bond with you in order to regulate, manage, and express their emotions (Goh, 2017). Establish this connection by observing them and getting to know them. Not only does this help you understand where your child is coming from, but it also helps you understand the logic behind their emotional expression. You can bond with your child in a number of ways, including by spending quality time together and demonstrating interest in their lives. However, for young kids, a surefire way to establish a link is to comfort them in times of distress. When things aren't going all that well, give your child a hug to let them know you are there and that you care.

Punishment Isn't Always the Answer

Discipline is essential, but overly harsh or punitive measures will prove not only ineffective but will also be to your child's detriment in the long run. These disciplinary techniques teach your child that expression is bad and may lead to further distress or punishment. Consequently, emotions become repressed, which is incredibly damaging to your child's development. Put punishment on the back burner and lend a hand to help your child find an effective way of understanding and working through their emotions. More importantly, find a way that is healthy, and that will provide your child with an improvement in their problem-solving skills. Help them brainstorm a basic approach or method. Then, give them the time and space to implement it so that they can see how it works. If it proves effective to some extent, encourage them to revise and refine it so that it works better for them. Make sure they understand that they must do this on their own.

The Two *P*'s: Praise and Practice

Expression comes naturally to some kids, while others may find it more daunting. Regardless of your child's predisposition to emotional sharing, remember to praise them for their efforts. Do this when they have succeeded, as well as when they haven't quite managed to communicate what they had intended. Praising your child even for trying sends the message that emotional expression is a good thing and that it makes you feel proud of them. At the same time, make sure your child knows that the perfect means of expression won't be attained on the first try, if at all. It is a skill they will hone for the rest of their lives. However, practice will get them as close to perfect as possible, and they should do their best.

Actionable Activities

Remember that children learn better when they are engaged and when they have the opportunity to attempt EI practices more than once. With that in mind, let's take a look at some activities we can engage in with our children to help them along the road to healthy emotional expression. As always, keep your child's temperament and preferences in mind and facilitate activities that will speak to them most.

Daily Activities

These activities are ones you can seamlessly integrate into your household's ordinary routine. You can do an emotion check-in at the start and end of each day or encourage your children to take up an activity that will act as an outlet for emotional expression. Chapter 5 covers examples of these activities. Whatever it is your child chooses, help them carve out some time in the day for its execution, and make sure that they stick to these activities. Once they have become a part of your child's routine, you can try to join in a few times to observe your child as they express themselves.

Literacy Activities

Use books as the basis for the identification of emotions and show your child how certain feelings can be expressed. When a character's experiences are described or illustrated, ask your child how you think this will make them feel. In other instances, ask them what they think the motivating feeling behind a behavior is, and ask them whether they think this expression is appropriate. Start these activities with your child's favorite book and steadily expand to other written works.

Musical Activities

Expose your child to different genres of music and ask them how each one makes them feel. Once they have a good grasp on the types of emotions, elevate the activity by having you and your child express these feelings while listening to the music. You don't necessarily need to dance. You can just move about or change your bodily posture to reflect how the different compositions make each of you feel.

Activities Using Drama

For more sophisticated exercises, consider crafting and using puppets to help your child act out scenarios involving different types of emotional expression. However, if you want something less intricate, refer back to Chapter 5, which describes the activity of emotional charades. In addition to this, you can craft an activity in which you mimic different emotions using your face and have your child guess what you are representing. Where the charades activity is based around situations, using only your face keeps the stakes and difficulty low, making it ideal for younger kids.

Movement Activities

These activities enable you to use your body to demonstrate to your child how different types of expressions look. Spend some time outdoors and, giving your child prompts, have them physically inhabit the expression of certain emotions. For something more complex, use mime to get your kids to play out different emotional scenarios. You can also simply have them shake their bodies out and assume whichever position or posture best depicts what they are feeling at that moment.

Games

Chapter 5 contains a number of diverting games you can use to help your children sharpen their skills of expression. An alternative game you can play involves you and your child or your child and one of their friends. In the game of mirrors, an emotion is assigned to one player, who must then do a series of actions and say some words expressing this feeling. Your child mimics their partner's actions and, in doing so, gains valuable experience in showing emotions to the world.

The Arts

Finally, grab a bunch of colors and ask your kids to tell you which feelings each of the shades elicits. For something a bit more concrete, create a time in which your child can draw freely and without interruption. Ask them to draw their day in emotions. This activity facilitates the double-whammy of self-awareness and the exploration of expression. This doesn't have to be limited to drawing, as your child can use any type of craft to construct and communicate their experiences.

Helping Your Child Manage Difficult Feelings

If our children know how to express their emotions effectively and honestly, that's amazing. However, not all expressions are appropriate for all situations, and not all kids know how to adjust the scale of their emotions depending on the situation. The ability to do this is a skill that our kids must learn and is one that forms an incredibly important part of EI.

This ability is that of self-regulation, which forms part of a constellation of skills, all of which contribute to an individual's ability to control and manage different aspects of their personhood. For our purposes here, we are most concerned with emotional self-regulation, which is the ability to manage emotions and their connected thoughts and behaviors. When effectively self-regulating, a person can retain this control without having to shift their focus from the task or situation at hand. It's important that we distinguish between self-regulation and self-control. The former involves cognitive as well as behavioral abilities, while the latter is largely a social skill that steers a person away from inappropriate behavior (Brandwein, 2022).

Self-regulation is important for a number of reasons, not the least of which is that it allows our children to process events before calmly and logically deciding on a behavior to exhibit in response. Moreover, this ability helps our children to calm themselves down when needed and to become more emotionally, cognitively, and behaviorally flexible. If your child is able to self-regulate, they will take changes and setbacks in stride and won't allow these occurrences to hinder their progress or development. Finally, teaching this skill has an influence on other aspects of EI. More specifically, it helps our children adopt and maintain prosocial behaviors, which help cultivate healthy, happy relationships.

Despite the importance of self-regulation, it isn't something that our minds possess from birth. This skill must be taught, acquired, and cultivated. However, as with any ability, picking it up isn't necessarily easy. But if we know how beneficial self-regulation can be, why do some children struggle with it? The answer, quite simply, is that our children are overburdened. Many modern parents want to set their children up for success by pushing them to acquire skills that are too complex for their age. We push our kids to do too much, too fast, for fear that they will start too late and subsequently fail in life. Additionally, kids nowadays aren't getting enough sleep, a phenomenon that has been proven to be linked to a decrease in cognitive function and regulation.

Finally, all of this compounds and takes our young children away from playtime (Brandwein, 2022). As we know, free play is an experience that is essential to the development of important life skills. However, because our children are too busy with other pursuits, they don't get time to play. Even when they do, their engagement doesn't go deep enough to facilitate adequate learning. In the end, our children simply don't develop the emotional bandwidth to accommodate abilities like self-regulation.

Self-Regulation Strategies

Our knowledge of self-regulation is of no use if we do not possess the ability to translate this theory into practice. Luckily, despite the fact that self-regulation is not a natural-born quality, helping our children pick up this skill isn't terribly difficult. Strategies we can implement to help our kids build their self-regulatory abilities include the following:

- Taking things in turns: Help your child learn cooperation and sharing by using timers. By allocating a specific duration to an activity, your child will learn when it is time to wrap things up, even if they want to continue. At the same time, they will come to understand that their actions affect others as well.

- Patience and waiting: Teach patience and impulse control through distraction. Over time, your child will learn to shift their focus from a long wait and the frustrations that could come with it.

- Breathing exercises: Breathing eliminates agitation by moving your brain out of the state induced by a stress response. This strategy can be as simple as taking five deep breaths, but it can be made more complex by combining breathing with visualization. You can use the "rainbow breath" exercise for this. Starting with your hands at your sides, inhale. Raise your arms and envision tracing a rainbow in the air with your fingers. Repeat the exercise, continuing the visualization. By attaching a visual element, you engage your child's imagination while also providing the calming effects of deep breathing.

- Verbalize vowels: Alternating between "ah" and "oh," breathe deeply and sound out the vowel as you exhale. Maintain the sound for as long as you can. This activity helps to conclude the stress response and provides the same calming effects as the breathing exercise.

- Identifying emotionality and impulsivity: Recognize visual cues that denote emotions and needs. Regulate their effects by evaluating them objectively and nonchalantly. In doing so, your child learns the reality of their emotions without becoming invested in or offended by their presence.

- Venting: This strategy is all about catharsis. Release pent-up feelings through movements, verbalizations, or any other means of powerful, lightening expression.

- Reflecting: When your child has experienced some emotional distress, sit down with them, and examine how they felt before the event, how it changed their emotional state in the moment, and how they feel after its conclusion. Examine what they did right and on which aspects of their response they can work.

- Cooling down: Similar to the reflecting exercise, this can be performed when your child has undergone some distress. Give them a cool drink of water, have them splash some cold water in their face, or cool down in another way. This takes them out of their moment of agitation and gives their nervous system a sobering shock.

Self-Regulation Activities

In addition to the strategies and exercises mentioned above, you can participate in a few fun, simple activities with your child. Take inspiration from the activities listed below:

- Get outside and smell the flowers for a touch of natural centering.

- Get down on all fours and facilitate catharsis by moving like an animal.

- Brighten up everyone's day by holding a smiling competition.

- Release frustrations by clenching your fists and tightening your muscles before relaxing all over.

- Play some mindful games where your child focuses on the moment so they can connect their physical behaviors to their sensory experiences.

Finally, we conclude the self-regulatory learning experience by looking at some science-based strategies we can employ to enhance these abilities in our children. We can start by helping them realize that this regulation is in service of a larger goal: a higher level of EI. Help them understand that gaining control now will help them in the long run and will set them up for success. We can achieve this by connecting the theory behind self-regulation to scenarios our kids encounter on a regular basis. For example, show them that they already possess a measure of impulse control by having the ability to stand in line for something or to wait until Christmas morning before opening their presents.

You can make the process easier by being upfront with your child about the difficulty of self-regulation. By doing this, they won't feel bad if they falter and will learn the quality of motivation to push through when self-regulation seems too difficult to achieve. This ease is increased by having a clear direction in which they want to develop. Similar to setting goals, determine what your child hopes to achieve through self-regulation and how they will manage to attain these results. Round out this part of the process by explaining to your child that while self-regulation is a skill they can acquire in the present, they will spend their lives maintaining it. Highlight its benefits once more to ensure they don't become discouraged.

Finally, make learning accessible to them by making it fun and by providing them with activities and games that will teach them these skills. In doing so, you stimulate more than just your child's regular cognitive learning centers. Moreover, you can tailor the learning experience according to their learning style and preferences. The very last thing to do is practice a bit of acceptance. Realize that while you can provide your child with structure, guidance, and support, this journey is very much their own. In order for them to gain control, you must first learn to let go of them.

The Importance of the Occasional Cry

The purpose of this chapter is to help us learn how to identify and embrace big emotions. Though opinions may differ, I'd wager that the overwhelming majority of parents would agree that crying falls under the umbrella of "big." Crying is an integral part of the child-rearing experience, especially if we consider the fact that sometimes it's alright for our kids to shed some tears.

This consideration begins with understanding the difference between the cries of an infant and a toddler. On a foundational level, these cries are relatively similar, as our children will use tears as a means of expressing discomfort, pain, or anger (Macklin, 2022). However, this is where the resemblance stops. Having to deal with our children's crying is similarly divergent. In infants, crying doesn't always have to be attended to. Naturally, if they are hungry or ill, it's important for us to help them resolve the issue and put an end to the tears. In toddlerhood, it's essential for us to determine why our kids are crying. Though not every situation requires a resolution on our part (more on that in a moment), this is a formative stage of our children's lives, and we must help them work through difficult emotions and situations as best we can.

For infants, crying is instinctual and functions as a signal of experience. Children of this age's cries are communicative and help alert parents to everything from hunger to pain to a desire for attention. By contrast, toddlers crying results from their sudden ability to perceive complex emotions and experiences. Crucially, this perception does not arise concurrently with the ability to understand what it is they are experiencing. Where before, as infants, they cried because of simple things such as hunger or fatigue, they now cry because they are aware of the different sensations that come along with experiences such as these. Yet they can't do anything about it, and their only way of coping is to cry. Additionally, toddlers' fears and needs also become more complex. However, given their limited skill set, this may also be dealt with through tears.

For all the different reasons that a child may cry, there is one perspective we can take with regards to this type of emotional expression: crying is okay. This view does have a number of reasons attached to it as well, not the least of which is avoiding unhealthy resolution techniques. If we try to put an end to our children's tears every time they fall, we may, in fact, be reinforcing or unwittingly encouraging manipulative behaviors. Moreover, if we do whatever we can to make them stop crying, we are denying them the opportunity to learn a new emotional skill or to demonstrate something such as self-regulation or self-awareness.

It's alright to let your child cry if it means that they are undergoing an educational experience. If you refuse to entertain their manipulative tears, they will learn that their behavior is not only wrong but will prove ineffective when utilized against you. In addition to this, we should let our kids cry if it provides them with the chance to employ some of their EI. Let their tears flow so that they may release negative, pent-up emotions, and so that they may work through whatever it is they are feeling. Sometimes, crying is the default response to being overwhelmed by emotion. If you allow your child enough time, they will calm down, see that they possess the skills they need to diffuse the situation, and do just this. Given enough time and practice, they will come to this conclusion earlier, potentially even before they well up.

While crying can certainly be helpful, there are certain scenarios in which we should try to help our children out of this state of emotional distress. We have touched on these already, particularly as they present in infants. Emotional distress is a natural part of life and is the best way for our children to learn how to manage their emotions. However, this type of distress doesn't always limit its effects to the realms of the mind and heart. Sometimes, our children may cry because they are experiencing genuine physical distress, such as illness or injury. In younger kids, crying may intensify when they try to communicate an urgent need. If our children are experiencing true fears or panic, or if they find themselves crumbling under the weight of their feelings, it's time for us to step in.

Crying is a good thing, but as parents, we mustn't lull ourselves into a sense of complacency when it comes to tears. In some instances, our children can work through the crying, but in others, they need our immediate and full attention. Even when the crisis has been somewhat inflated, don't leave your child to their own devices. While you can't solve their problems, you can support and comfort them, letting them know that you are always there should they need you.

Naturally, if crying is as advantageous as it has been presented here, there ought to be some benefits we can point to in support of this type of expression. First, we start with the fact that crying in and of itself is a form of emotional expression and, as such, helps our children work on their emotional management as well as embrace those big, messy feelings that characterize life. By crying, our kids gain experience with new means of conveying their emotions and make strides towards learning self-regulation. Next, we see the benefit tied to this expression, which is catharsis. Crying is a release, and along with tears, our children expel emotional weights that are too heavy for them to carry. While crying may not always solve your child's problem, it will make them feel a bit better. This brings us to the final, most scientific benefit of all. That catharsis we just learned about is not just an act of expulsion but of excretion as well. When our kids cry, their bodies get rid of the hormone cortisol, which we know plays a key role in the natural stress response. Effectively, your child is crying their way back to a homeostatic internal environment (Lively, 2018).

Knowing what to do when confronted with a crying child is the final step towards helping them learn about emotional management and control. However, along with these tips, we should be aware that there are certain things we should avoid at all costs. When responding to your child's cries, try to take the following into consideration:

- First and foremost, ensure that your child isn't crying because they are injured or ill. If this is the case and you can treat it yourself, do so. If you are unsure of the cause or the solution, consult a medical professional.

- Talk to your child about what is upsetting them if the cause is not easily visible. Ask them why they are crying, what they are feeling, and what they believe could help. Come up with a collaborative solution to help them through this difficulty.

- Remind them that it is perfectly healthy to cry and that what they are feeling will pass in time.

- Consider who your child is, what their temperament is like, and how they respond to stimuli when devising a solution to their problems. Help them through it in a way that will appeal to their minds the most. If you find that you can't calm them down or help them solve their problem, sit with them, comfort them, and offer your support.

- It is essential that you remember to take care of your own emotional well-being, especially if your child cries often. Lean on your support network to get some time to yourself in which to rest and reset. The stabler your internal environment, the better the help you will be able to offer your child.

- Don't bottle up your emotions. If you feel saddened or overwhelmed when your child cries, consider shedding a few tears along with them. This shows them how natural the practice is and might provide the both of you with some much-needed release.

By contrast, try to avoid the following responses when your child's emotions spill out through their eyes:

- Never get physical with a crying child. Not only may this worsen their emotional state, but you may cause them serious injury. Step back, take a breath, and calm down before you return to your child.

- Don't dismiss your child's emotions because you may not have time for them. Doing so will invalidate your child's feelings, which in turn may lead them to begin repressing their emotions.

- Don't attempt to distract your child from what has upset them. Though this may act as a bandage in the moment, it will not heal the emotional wound, and you will find yourself reliving this experience at some point down the line.

- Don't ignore your children's cries in the hopes that they will go away. They won't.

- Be careful not to rush your child through the process of understanding and dealing with their emotions. The better they understand this experience and their response to it, the better they will be able to formulate a plan for the future. Denying them the space and time to figure things out will undoubtedly lead them to repeat this behavior time and time again.

Finally, if you are unsure of how to provide comfort or assistance when your child finds themselves in times of distress, use the following sample phrases to construct your own verbal responses:

- "I can see that you are having a hard time with this."

- "It's okay to feel this way."

- "I'm here if you need me."

- "Let's take a step back, breathe, and try again."

- "Yes, that experience really was [insert emotion here]."

- "This is a safe space."

- "Do you think there's a way to solve this problem?"

- "Would you like me to help you find a way to fix this?"

- "Do you remember when you felt like this before? What did you do then?"

- "What can I do to help?"

Managing Your Own Emotions

We conclude this chapter by taking a look inward to determine the nature of our own internal emotional state. We have to ensure that we ourselves possess the ability to regulate and manage our emotions before we begin teaching our children these same skills. Knowing how to do this is part of the approach to calm parenting. This parenting technique recommends the following tips for staying in control and preventing your emotions from getting the best of you:

- Remain in possession of your power and authority: Your compulsion as a parent may be to deal with your child's behavior by getting them to behave according to your wishes. In doing so, you shift your focus from yourself to them and make yourself vulnerable. If your kids know your emotional state is dependent on their actions, this empowers them to do what they like. Instead of trying to elicit something from your children, turn your attention inward and determine what you need to deal with the situation while retaining emotional control at the same time.

- Walk away (for now): Distressing situations don't exactly trigger the most logical parts of your brain. When you see your child, their behaviors, and their actions through the haze of frustration, you are more likely to lose control and meddle out punishments that are far too harsh. Even if you don't punish your kids, your response in the heat of the moment may not be the most emotionally intelligent. Remain in control by walking away from the situation for a while until you have calmed down enough to view it logically and objectively.

- Don't let emotions guide emotions: Always remember that your feelings don't necessarily stem from logical cognitive function. To avoid impulsivity and loss of control, approach your emotions from a perspective of reason and rationality. By allowing cognition to take the lead, you will be able to handle emotional situations effectively, positively, and comprehensively.

- Self-regulation, not self-judgment: You cannot handle your children's emotions and behaviors without judgment or condemnation if you cannot do the same thing for yourself. Be kind to yourself and allow yourself the same kind of emotional recognition you afford your children. Recognize your own emotions as valid and deal with them rather than pushing them aside. You have to understand and control your own internal state before you can help your children work on theirs.

- Be fully present: Whether you are dealing with your own emotions or helping your children manage theirs, you have to be fully present. In order to work through your feelings thoroughly and in a constructive manner, you have to focus the entirety of your attention on the situation at hand. Consciously shut out external stimuli and distractions so that you can focus all of your emotion and cognitive power on the experience you are working through in that moment.

Our journey towards raising emotionally intelligent children is nearly complete. Before we reach the finish line, however, it is imperative that we have a grasp on our own emotions, and that we support and enable our children to gain this same level of control over their own. At times, this may prove difficult, especially as your child matures and experiences feelings of ever-increasing magnitude. In those moments, take a step back and think of the big picture. Embracing feelings big and small is a key component of EI. Once our kids have their own emotions down pat, they can expand their focus to working with the feelings of the people in their lives.

Chapter 7:

Walking in Others' Shoes

Empathy is about finding echoes of another person in yourself. –Mohsin Hamid

Of the five basic tenets that make up emotional intelligence, perhaps none is so easily or practically implementable as that of empathy. Listening to others and truly understanding what they wish to share with you about their experiences is one of the best skills your child can acquire in their lifetime. Once our children have gained a working knowledge of how to regulate their own internal environment, they can enrich their relationships through the practice of empathy. In addition to helping your child make friends, being empathetic has the potential to take them far in life.

What Is Empathy?

In the very first chapter of this book, we examined empathy as part of the concept of EI. For a quick refresher, refer back to this chapter for the precise definition. Alternatively, just remember that being empathetic involves understanding the emotional experiences of the people in your life and having the ability to separate your own perspective on the matter from theirs. This skill is incredibly important and will help your child succeed in just about every relationship they have in life. However, teaching empathy is not entirely easy.

Don't let this discourage you, as the silver lining to this is that human beings are naturally predisposed to empathetic responses. In infants as young as 18 hours old, we can observe a response to the distress of other babies around them (Walsh & Walsh, 2019). In the first years of life, your child's natural empathetic attributes will begin to manifest, laying the foundation for the development of this skill as they grow older. The emotional components of empathy will emerge first, with the cognitive components making their presence known by the time your child enters preschool.

While the foundational aspects of empathy start to emerge early in life, honing and perfecting this ability is not achieved overnight, if ever. Your child picks up empathy-related skills for the entirety of their life. The more experiences they have in terms of relationships, communication, and other EI activities, the more fully their empathetic skills will expand and refine. It is crucial that we keep the uniqueness of each child in mind as we guide them through the process of learning empathy. As with any other EI ability, some children will pick up the particulars of empathy relatively quickly, while the learning process will occur more steadily for others.

Acquiring empathy is also influenced by the nature of the emotional environments to which a child is exposed throughout their life. In more conducive, supportive contexts, empathy will thrive, while environments in which emotions are not dealt with or embraced will make this process more difficult. Keep in mind that your child will learn empathy at their own pace. Given how essential this skill is, you shouldn't rush learning empathy. The more secure children feel as they pick up empathetic abilities, the more likely they are to retain them.

Explaining the Concept

When you explain to your child what empathy is, you are effectively laying the groundwork for how they approach this ability and their method for learning it. As such, it is essential that we ensure our children have a comprehensive idea of what empathy is, conceptually speaking, as well as how it presents itself in practice. This explanation can be difficult, given how nebulous and nuanced empathy can be. Below, you will find an example script detailing the information you can impart when first introducing the concept. As always, use this as a framework only, adjusting it to your child's age, experience, environment, and relationships.

When sitting your child down to introduce empathy, explain to them that the empathetic process progresses in three distinct stages. Your child may feel them one after the other or may not feel more than one. This isn't cause for concern, as each stage exemplifies a different type of empathy. If your child has not demonstrated a tendency toward a specific type, cover each type. However, if your child has shown that they are more adept at cognitive empathy as opposed to emotional empathy, focus on that type to ensure the message is applicable to their life.

The explanation of empathy can be constructed as follows:

Imagine that your very best friend in the world has recently lost their pet. One day, as the two of you are sitting on the playground enjoying recess, your friend opens up to you about this experience.

When your brain switches over to empathy mode, the very first thing you may experience is the feeling that you understand exactly what they are feeling. This doesn't mean you have lost a pet yourself, but you know that your friend is sad and that they are hurting right now. You won't be as affected by the pet's passing as your friend is because it wasn't your pet, but you will understand that your friend is upset, and you can understand where these feelings come from.

If your friend's pain runs very deep, your brain may take the next step and make you feel the way they do. This is your brain telling you that the best way for you to make your friend feel better is to take on their experience for yourself. Despite the fact that your dog is fine (or that you don't even have one), you also feel like you have lost something and that someone you loved has gone from your life. Your brain is putting you in your friend's shoes so that you can understand them better.

The third and final stage of empathy is something that moves from your brain to your body. Your friend's story will make you feel so sad for them that you will feel like you have to do something to help them get through this emotional struggle. You might find that you remember a time when you felt a similar way and what made you feel better. If you do the same thing for your friend or something that is just as significant or personal, you might just be able to lift their spirits.

When you hear your friend telling you about their struggles, remember that they aren't necessarily asking you to solve their problem. Although you may want to help your friend in some way, you have to think about whether they are asking for a solution or just want someone to talk to. If there is something small you can do to help, go ahead. However, if your child doesn't ask you to fix everything, don't go out of your way to try to help. Listen to them, let them know you are there for them, and support them through this difficult time.

In addition to using this script as an example of how you can explain empathy to your child, you can provide them with actual examples of this practice in action. Similar to your customization of the explanation, use the following scenarios as a basis for crafting examples that will connect with your child:

- It's the start of a new school year, and you have a new classmate who spends recess without any friends. You feel bad that they are alone, and maybe you even go over there to invite them to join your friend group.

- You hear that someone in your class is having a hard time at home because their parents are getting divorced. While you can't relate exactly, you bring them a chocolate bar the next day to let them know they can talk to you and that you are thinking of them.

- Your sister is upset because you left some of your toys in the living room. Initially, you are annoyed because you said that you would put them away later. However, if you think about it some more, you realize that the living room is a shared space, and your toys are cluttering the space, making it difficult for your sister to use the room like she wants to. You understand where she is coming from and admit to yourself that if she had done the same, you would have felt just as upset with her.

The Importance of Empathy

Helping our children develop the skill of empathy is hugely important. Not only does it enable them to strengthen their EI, but it also provides them with a variety of life skills. What makes empathy so compelling and beneficial is that its effects can be felt all throughout childhood and last well into your child's adult years. Because empathy is learned over the course of a lifetime, we are continually reaping the fruits of this practice for as long as we put it to use.

Starting with childhood, we can identify some of empathy's benefits as follows:

- Empathy opens children's eyes to the importance of emotional connection and support, and enables them to reach out for help when needed.

- The ability to inhabit different perspectives to understand and work through problems has been linked to elevated academic performance (Lee, 2019).

- Children understand that some behaviors hurt others and what the extent of this pain can be. In doing so, empathizing can help prevent bullying.

- Empathetic children are secure in themselves and understand what they need to succeed, which improves their learning abilities.

- Through understanding others' perspectives and experiences, children become more tolerant and accepting.

- Having the ability to work through emotions helps children keep track of and maintain their mental health.

If the practice of empathy is sustained throughout adulthood, you can expect your child to enjoy a number of benefits later in life. These include the following:

- Lee (2019) has identified flexibility of perspective and approach as enabling adults to excel in professional environments.

- Empathetic adults understand emotions better and, as such, are able to build and sustain happy, healthy, long-term relationships.

- Empathy sets adults up to excel in leadership positions through their ability to execute diplomacy, compromise, and support.

- Conflict resolution is learned alongside the knowledge of handling other people's emotions.

- Living a life in which emotions are understood, and logic is applied empathetically leads to lower levels of stress.

Empathy Milestones

Empathy develops throughout your child's entire life, and with each year that passes, their abilities become more refined and more specific to their lived experience. While competent empathizing isn't a skill with which we are necessarily born, the human mind does possess certain qualities that enable us to pick up the particulars of this practice. We know that each child will become empathetic at their own pace. However, there are certain age-bound milestones we can look out for to monitor our children's progress.

The First Weeks of Life

At the very start of your child's life, they won't possess very many demonstrable qualities tied to empathy. That being said, your newborn can display a measure of empathy through their response. This is particularly noticeable in times of distress when the perception of another infant's sadness or stress will trigger cries in your own child. At this age, your child can also form responses to emotional cues, even if they are unaware they are doing so. Newborns wish to interact with the people in their lives, so they will respond best to open, inviting, and engaged facial expressions, as well as tones of voice that reflect these qualities. By contrast, cold, distant, or uninterested faces, and voices will, in turn, shut down your child's interactions. Eye contact is especially important here, as your child will learn that looking at something draws attention. Pretty soon, you will see the first demonstration of emotional emulation as your child turns their head to follow your gaze so that they can know where your attention goes (Dewar, 2015).

Six to Eight Weeks

Moving into the first months, the edges of your baby's mouth will start to creep upward. Initially, this tentative grin won't be connected to happiness or humor. Instead, sleeping infants crack a smile when they alleviate feelings of gassiness. However, over the course of six to eight weeks, your positive engagement in those early days will begin to show its impact. Known as a social smile, your infant will begin to attach a smile to the experience of genuine emotions. When you amuse them or when they feel happy, your baby will smile up at you. It is crucial to remember their perceptive skills at this age, as this smile can also be elicited through positive, friendly interactions and expressions. Additionally, your six-to-eight-week-old may start smiling without being prompted. In the absence of positive stimuli, your baby's smile communicates an intention: To make you happy and receive a grin in return.

Eight to Ten Months

Near the end of the first year, your child is much more perceptive. At this age, they start to engage in sympathy, which acts as a precursor for empathetic behaviors (Dewar, 2015). When they perceive someone they care for to be in distress, they will attempt some sort of response. This may manifest as verbalizations, gestures, facial expressions, or other behaviors intended to help them understand another person's emotional state. Note that at this age, emotions are still quite heavy concepts. Even if your child demonstrates these positive interpersonal behaviors, this doesn't mean they understand emotions just yet. They will shy away or cower if presented with an emotion that is too big or too scary for them to handle. These are early days; don't expect too much, too fast.

One Year

At 12 months, your child will begin to learn empathy through the use of mimicry and imagination. In a practice known as social play, infants will start to concoct more elaborate and complex scenarios when playing with peers and caregivers. They do this as a learning mechanism. When they play by themselves, they have carte blanche to do what they please. However, when another person is involved, it becomes a collaborative effort, and your child must learn to pay attention to their playmate's intentions and actions, as well as their behavioral, visual, and emotional cues. They learn to consider others.

14 to 18 Months

Between the first two years of life, your child will pick up an important new attribute: helpfulness. Infants between these ages are likely to provide you with simple help without needing prompting. They may pick things up for you if you drop them or bring you something you are looking for. The most significant development occurs at the end of this period when your child makes what is known as an "empathic breakthrough" (Dewar, 2015). Where before, their decisions were largely egocentric, focused on aligning behaviors and choices with their own preferences, they will now remember your likes and dislikes and take them into consideration. Even if your child dislikes a specific type of chocolate, if they know you like it, they will most likely bring it to you when selecting treats for the two of you.

24 to 36 Months

At two years old, your child is able to pick up on cues and respond accordingly. Through observation, your child is able to suss out how you are feeling (more or less) and behave in a manner they believe is helpful. If you show signs of sadness, they will notice and come give you a hug. Though the most effective stimuli are still verbal expressions of your emotional state, your child is learning to pick up on nonverbal cues to dictate their behavior in interpersonal interactions. All the while, your child's brain is working to expand upon the skills learned in their first year and a-half. Each of the abilities they gained during this time is continuously developed and refined, as your child is learning all the time.

Part of this learning manifests as the formation of a "theory of mind." Near the time of your child's second birthday, they come to the realization that people are different from one another. They realize that their friends, parents, and family members all have their own inner lives and experiences. More importantly, your two-year-old's theory of mind allows them to understand that the state of these inner lives isn't just different when it comes to other people, but that their states will differ from your child's (Matthews, 2019)

Four Years

As a preschooler, your child experiences only one significant development in their fourth year. At this age, they learn the invaluable skill of seeing things from another's point of view.

This ability is fundamental to the practice of empathy and effectively paves the way for them to expand upon their skills in the future.

Five Years

In their fifth year, your child will be able to gauge which reactions and behaviors are appropriate for the situations in which they find themselves. Additionally, they will become increasingly emotional and may express the desire to talk about some of these feelings with you. If they are emotionally healthy, these conversations will contain significant depth. Along with this comes the desire to be seen as a fully-fledged member of society at large, or even just the household, if they operate on a smaller scale. Five-year-olds want to be recognized, both for their personhood as well as for their emotional experiences.

Six Years

The final milestone to look out for is an important one. At six years old, your child has the ability to recognize, analyze, and interpret social cues. This skill will be used for the rest of their lives and involves paying attention. In the same way, you observe your kids, they observe the people around them. In doing so, they are able to pick up on gestures, expressions, vocal cues, and behaviors that signal a person's emotional state. They will then use this information to formulate an appropriate response and dictate their behavior for as long as they remain in that situation.

Helping Your Child Recognize and Validate Emotions in Others

Though it's useful for us to know what empathy is and how we can look out for it in our children, this information is of little use to our kids if it stays trapped in our minds. It's up to us to help our children along the path to becoming empathy-enabled people. This process won't be quick, but that doesn't mean it has to be difficult. To help our children understand and respond to the emotions of others, we can take the following actionable steps:

- Lead by example: Never to be counted out; behavioral and emotional modeling show up once more. Show your child what kind and empathetic behavior looks like so that they can see how the theory behind the practice is put to use. If you apply the principles of empathy to your interactions with your child, they will experience firsthand what it feels like to be understood, and supported. Once they have a grasp of this, they can begin to mimic these behaviors in their own lives.

- Discuss the nature of empathy: This method is relatively easy, as you can explain the concept of empathy in words that your child will understand. When describing how emotions are viewed, processed, and used as part of empathizing, ensure that you use examples that feature within your child's emotional vocabulary.

- Help them unpack and understand their feelings: Listen to your child when their feelings get the better of them and try to help them pin down what exactly it is they are experiencing. Additionally, help them understand where these feelings come from. When they have encounters in which other people become upset, discuss what happened and see if your child can determine why the other person felt that way. By helping them do this unpacking to start off, you can teach them the basics of the practice before they start empathizing on their own.

- Get imaginative: Sit them down and ask them to imagine what others may be feeling in any given situation. Help your child construct hypothetical situations in which they can practice identifying emotions and brainstorm ways for them to empathize with the characters in these scenarios. For something more visually stimulating, practice this with the characters in their favorite film or television show. Have them decipher cues that might point to the characters' feelings, and ask your child why they believe the person feels that way, as well as how they would go about addressing their situation.

- Open up: Being open and honest with your child about your feelings and experiences will help them understand that other people have emotional lives that are just as rich and complex as their own. Provide them with comprehensive descriptions, as this will clue them into the behavioral and emotional cues that characterize another person's state of mind.

- Empathize rather than apologize: More often than not, we feel compelled to teach our children to apologize because it is expected or appropriate. However, if our kids apologize simply out of habit without understanding why it is necessary, their words ring hollow. We have to teach our children to understand why apologies are needed, as this will help them grasp the fact that their actions have an effect on the emotions of others.

- Give them a chance to try again: Employing empathetic behavior isn't easy, even if your child is naturally adept at handling emotions. So, when your child falters as they attempt empathy, encourage them to keep going and to try again. Help them identify the mistake they made and how it affected others. Then, in the interest of trying again, help them find a way to rectify this mistake and practice empathy.

- Teach the empathetic response: Through discussion or modeling, teach your child to respond to bad or distressed behavior with curiosity instead of anger or frustration. Encourage them to ask questions aimed at determining why the other person has responded that way, what elicited this reaction, and what your child can do to help. For the latter question, it is helpful to remember that assistance is sometimes a physical action, such as a hug or solving a problem. At other times, the best way to empathize is to listen and let the other person know they are heard and supported.

- Remember the role of the Internet: If possible, try to have your child spend some time away from screens. Through in-person interactions, your child will have the best chance to practice their empathy skills and learn about the complexity of emotions as they present themselves to other people. Ensure that, while your child can certainly spend some time online, there is a measure of balance between this and the time they spend with real people.

- Make your kid a hero: Practicing empathy can be intimidating, particularly when it involves standing up for yourself or helping others through times of emotional difficulty. Through a combination of behavioral modeling, encouragement, support, and emotional management, you can equip your child with all the tools they need to come to their own rescue. If you're lucky, they may be able to do the same for someone else, too.

Some General Tips

- Set high yet reasonable standards for your child's emotional behavior and make empathy a priority.

- Provide your child with plenty of learning opportunities as well as chances to demonstrate their emotional abilities.

- Help your child understand that emotional struggle isn't unique to them or the people in their life.

- Teach your child emotional self-regulation.

- Help your child build their social skills and incorporate empathy from the start.

- Don't shame or chastise your child for mistakes; help them identify and correct their mistakes.

- Foster open and honest discussions about difficult subjects so that your child may learn about the realities of the world.

- Enable your child to empathize by teaching them the importance and value of difference as well as of similarity.

Key Empathy-Building Strategies: An Age-Appropriate Guide

When you teach your child empathy, remember that you are dealing with complex, abstract emotional concepts. Comprehending this may prove difficult, especially for younger children. In order to make the process easier and to ensure that your child understands what you teach them, divide the learning process into periods of time. When your child reaches the age assigned to each period, employ the strategies that are appropriate to help them build up their empathizing abilities.

Three to Five Years

Between these two ages, strategies are very much aimed at practicality and involve ordinary aspects of your child's life. You can help your toddler acquire the basics of empathy by building their emotional vocabulary. Use the people around them as examples, and help them label and describe the emotions they observe. Tap into the power of observation by teaching your child about body language and visual and non-verbal cues. Show them, someone, who is clenching their jaw and who wears a deep grimace. From there, look for other clues to determine whether they are in pain or are feeling frustrated.

You can also use a more artistic and creative approach. Using books, films, shows, and music as references, ask your child to help you spot emotions in characters, descriptions, and lyrics. For instance, if you watch a film together, pause at a point when you can see a character convey an emotion through body language. Ask your child to label and describe the emotion and perhaps even take a shot at guessing its origin. If a character delivers a particularly emotive line, pause again and ask your child to label that emotion as well. Ask them what they think that experience feels like and how the character's emotional state has changed in the last few minutes or scenes.

If your child (or you) likes to do some crafting, create an emotional first-aid kit. You can place items in this kit that your child identifies as comforting and would like to have in times of distress. This can be anything from a bandage to a teddy bear to even some flowers. Keep the kit close at hand, and use it as a visual aid when teaching empathy. Explain to your child that they are the human version of the first-aid kit and that the items inside the box are the emotional skills they can use to practice empathy.

Five to Seven Years

When your child reaches the age at which they start going to school, your empathy-teaching strategies will still partially play to their senses. You can use the game of emotion charades to help them expand their emotional vocabulary while simultaneously demonstrating the expression of certain emotions. In addition to this, visual aids will still come in handy at this age, as your child may have difficulty distinguishing between similar emotions as well as those that are slightly more complex.

Between five and seven, your main focus should be broadening your child's horizons. Give them ample opportunity to meet and engage with people from different cultures and backgrounds. Encourage them to make friends with kids whose families look different from their own or whose beliefs differ from your child's. This is a surefire way to introduce the concept of individuality as well as give your child real-life examples of how people differ.

More importantly, by fostering connections with a diverse array of people, your child learns to overcome differences and bond on common ground. It's important to avoid going overboard with exploration and exposure. Encourage your child to see what's out there and to start practicing empathy in everyday life. At the same time, make sure they know where their limits lie and the extent of the emotional weight they can carry. If your child does not set boundaries around their emotional life and empathizing abilities, they may start neglecting their own feelings in favor of tending to those of others. Help them set boundaries, specifically focused on knowing when to walk away and when to call in help.

Seven to Nine Years

From ages seven through nine, your child is constantly learning. Their minds are adjusting to the academic environment and, as such, are poised to soak up information. Use this to your advantage by teaching them empathy through literature and discussion. Structure it as a sort of oral book report in which you and your child discuss a book you have read together. Ask them to identify the characters' emotions in certain moments as well as their overall emotional development throughout the book. See if your child can point out moments of empathy in the plot, and ask them to describe what makes those particular actions empathetic.

At this age, your child will still be engaging in a fair amount of play. Use this time as a learning opportunity by having them play with friends and peers. From time to time, you can play along with them. Through these group play sessions, your child will learn how to collaborate and compromise, two skills that require them to understand another perspective, if not adopt it entirely. Along with learning through play, you can start to introduce your child to mindfulness techniques focused on kindness and love. For a basic exercise, guide them through a meditation in which they send out feelings of love to the people for whom they care. This is an introductory exercise used to determine whether your child is suited for the practice. If they are, you can gradually expand the range of emotions they focus on during meditation as well as introduce them to visualization exercises.

12 Years and Onwards

By the time your child becomes a preteen, they should have a firm grasp of what empathy entails and know how to handle and understand more complex emotions. This isn't to say that they will be perfectly empathetic beings; rather, the process should be smoother at this point. Encourage your child to use their stronger comprehension abilities by keeping up with the news. Through current events, your child will feel connected to the world and will have the opportunity to practice empathy for those people and groups mentioned in the news. You can help them put these feelings to good use by signing them up for community service and charity work so that they can practically engage in empathy.

As your child continues to grow, they will start to personalize their expressions of empathy. This is perfectly fine, as it means they care about the practice and wish to implement it in a way they know will be the most impactful. Encourage them to keep exploring and practicing, all the while reminding them that you are there for them if they need support or have new questions about what it means to be empathetic.

Statements of Empathy

Throughout the teaching process, it can be difficult to know which words to use to describe certain concepts or experiences. If your child is the one undergoing emotional distress, it can be equally difficult to know what to say, especially if we consider that this is your opportunity to demonstrate empathy in action.

In those moments when you are searching for words, use the following phrases to help you get the verbal ball rolling:

- If I were in your shoes, I would also be disappointed.

- I understand that you feel bad and that it hurts to feel this way.

- I have had similar feelings in the past.

- Thank you for being brave enough to share that with me; it must have been very difficult.

- I appreciate you sharing that with me, and I want you to know that I am here for you.

- Is this difficult for you to talk about?

- I understand that I have made you angry, and I thank you for being so honest with me.

- You're feeling some pretty big things. Is there anything I can do to help you right now?

- It sounds like you had a bad day today.

- You know, when [*insert experience here*] happened to me in the past, I felt [*insert emotion here*].

- I understand why you feel that way. I would, too, if I were you.

- It can be difficult to know what to do with friendships. We had these problems when I was a kid, too.

- I also find that I sometimes struggle with knowing what the right thing is to do.

- Do you want to hear about my worst day out as well?

- I understand that you feel bad because things didn't work out. I want you to know that I am nonetheless proud of you for trying.

- I know things are bad right now, and you want to give up, but…

- It seems that both of us are having a hard time right now.

- I feel as though I hurt your feelings. Do you think we can talk about it?

- I can't tell you what you should do, but I want you to know that I support your decision. I believe you can make this choice on your own.

Opportunities to Teach the Skill

There will be many opportunities for us to teach our children empathy from the time they are infants right up until they enter the adult world by themselves. Many of these opportunities will be unique to your circumstances and experiences and will require you to draw on your unique knowledge of your child. However, there are some experiences that are nearly universal, and that present a parent with an excellent, teachable moment.

Storytime

We have already explored the potential of using literary characters as examples for emotional identification and the demonstration of empathy. During storytime, you can employ these same practices but take it a step further by shifting the focus to include your child. Once you have discussed the characters' emotions and experiences, ask your child if they have ever felt a similar way. If they have, ask them what they did to make themselves feel better and what they would have preferred others do for them. Follow this up by asking them to imagine that one of their friends is having a similar experience and explaining what your child would do to help their friend through this troubling time.

Playtime

Play is an invaluable tool for the imparting of emotional wisdom, as it engages a number of your child's cognitive centers and skills. Help them learn empathy by making playtime an experience in which they feel safe and during which they can feel free to explore different emotions by acting out things they have seen or experienced. Join in and, without taking complete control, help them construct imaginary scenarios in which they get to practice taking turns, caring for others, and making use of their problem-solving skills.

Arguments With Siblings

While unpleasant for you as a parent, arguments between your children are perfect teachable moments. Start by acknowledging the validity of emotions on both sides. Then, talk to your kids about the impact their actions had on their siblings and imagine how they would have felt had the shoe been on the other foot. Finally, help them resolve the conflict as best they can. You must do this while maintaining a tone of neutrality. If you use overly angry or shaming language, you risk making things worse and teaching your child that their feelings are something they should feel ashamed of.

Trips to the Playground

What better place to engage in some educational people-watching than at the playground? A similar activity was described in Chapter 3, and you can use this for reference. When your child is at the playground, they have the opportunity to engage in social interactions, which they must learn to navigate. Help them understand why some of their friends may be upset or why they themselves became upset after a particular experience. Think not only of the reason for these emotions but also of ways to handle the situation that led to their appearance. If possible, resolve these situations at the playground to give your child a chance to employ their skills practically.

Setting Boundaries

Most of the time, we teach our kids about empathy in a controlled, safe environment. However, when they move into real-life scenarios, they may find this overwhelming and revert to emotionally unhelpful behaviors. It is essential that you set boundaries around emotional expression to help them understand what is appropriate and what is not. Validate their feelings; let them know you understand where they are coming from, but ensure they know why their actions were wrong. Help them get back on track by telling them that you cannot allow that behavior and providing them with a more positive alternative for the future.

Empathy can be a difficult thing to navigate, especially if we ourselves sometimes struggle with this skill. However, it is important that we keep trying and that we grow right alongside our children. Learning to be empathetic will take them far in life and will ensure that they enjoy a measure of emotional security and competence. As our journey of strengthening our children's EI approaches its end, we must consider what we haven't yet taught them and what we haven't learned about ourselves. If there is something we have missed, the best thing to do is to communicate the need for that knowledge and find a way to gain the insight we need.

Chapter 8:

Speaking Up and Listening Up

A child seldom needs a good talking to as a good listening to. –Robert Breault

Communication is the final piece we slot into place in order to complete the puzzle that is emotionally intelligent living. As part of helping our children cultivate their EI, we provide them with all the knowledge and tools they need to form lasting, healthy relationships. This process includes teaching them about the cornerstone of any good relationship: communication. As easy as this may sound, we must remember that communication is more than just simple expression. It also involves listening, knowing when to speak up and when to keep it to yourself, and knowing how to get your point across well. Our children must master each of these aspects in order to become good, healthy communicators.

Active Listening

The very first component of communication we take a look at is the one that enables us to receive information, and which informs our emotional response most significantly. This is none other than the practice of active listening, which involves focusing the entirety of your attention on the conversation you are part of in an attempt to fully comprehend the message being imparted by the speaker. When you practice active listening, you encourage positive conversation. You acknowledge the perspective of the speaker and pay close enough attention to be able to paraphrase the point they are making. In practice, active listeners provide speakers with both verbal and nonverbal cues signaling their focus and investment in the conversation (Oxford Learning, 2017).

In addition to the provision of these cues, active listeners perform this practice in three distinct stages. For children, they are as follows:

1. Hearing: When a child listens actively, they use an ability they already developed in the womb. During active listening, children use their sense of hearing to tune into the words of the person speaking to them. This marks the first shift in attention. However, it is crucial to note that hearing does not guarantee comprehension or retention. Rather, it is merely an acknowledgment of the sensory stimulus being thrown their way.

2. Listening: As the name suggests, listening is quite an important part of being an active listener. The detection of noises is an ability that develops early in life, and along with this comes the ability to attach meaning to these noises. This is what listening effectively is. We hear the sounds coming from the outside world and attach significance to them so that we can understand their message or intention. Active listening moves from hearing to the identification of verbal cues, such as inflections, changes in pitch, and tone. This is listening, as children look for meaning in the sounds coming to them from another person. Doing so actively also means sustaining this listening for extended periods of time.

3. Attention: Being able to focus on the present moment is a skill that children develop as they grow up. This

starts with being easily distractible and evolves to include multiple stimuli and activities until it settles into fully integrated attention at the age of five (Johnson, 2022). Crucially, not all children will develop their attention abilities at the same rate. However, when it comes to active listening, our child will take the meaning they've attached to the sounds from the speaker and focus their full attention on interpreting it. This means that their focus isn't diverted to anything else, and they can throw their full cognitive and emotional weight behind analyzing and responding to the conversation.

If we understand how much goes into being an active listener, then surely it stands to reason that there are benefits to be gained from all this cognitive effort. If you made this assumption, you would be entirely correct, as the most important benefit of active listening is the impact it has on our interpersonal relationships. By focusing the entirety of our attention on the people around us as they are speaking with us, we can foster deeper, more profound connections. Additionally, active listening helps us function more empathetically, as it enables us to validate and accept other people's emotional experiences.

Along with this positive impact on our lives, other benefits of active listening include:

- Heightened levels of autonomy and elevated EI.

- Improved resourcefulness and the strengthening of critical thinking skills.

- Better performance in collaborative situations.

- By paying full attention during interactions with others, fewer things get lost in translation, and we can avoid misunderstandings.

- Increased performance and a stronger work ethic.

Active Listening Skills

Much like any other skill linked to EI, active listening is something that must be taught and cultivated. Anyone can listen, but doing so intentionally and with emotional wherewithal may not come all that naturally. While your child's active listening skills will evolve and expand over the course of their lives, there are a few core practices you can teach them in preparation for the complexity down the road.

The first skill to teach your child is reflection, which allows them to observe the communication they receive and reconfigure it in a way that makes the most sense for them. When your child looks back on what they have been told, they can begin their reflection by paraphrasing it using words from their emotional vocabulary. As they restate this for themselves, they can add a sort of emotional clause at the end of the sentence. After paraphrasing the facts of the situation, tack on a tentative emotional conclusion. For example, your child can say that one of their friends' siblings took their friend's toy, and this made your child's friend angry.

Supplement the comprehension that comes with reflection by teaching your child to summarize. Often, when large quantities of information are communicated to them, your child may be unable to process the emotional undertones of this information. They can make it easier to understand by compressing the information and distilling it down to its key points. In doing so, they lay it out in a way that will be most conducive to their comprehension.

Your child can further deepen their understanding by ensuring that the communication isn't one-sided. They can do this by asking questions that will help them understand where the speaker is coming from as well as the emotions behind the experience they are sharing. By asking questions, your child affirms their intention to truly understand the speaker as well as their emotional investment in the conversation.

Round out your child's fundamental active listening skills by teaching them the power of nonverbal, physical cues. Through open body language, your child can communicate their willingness to be part of the conversation as well as encourage the speaker to share their experience. These cues don't have to be particularly elaborate or sophisticated. Something as simple as eye contact or quietly nodding can help keep the conversation flowing freely.

These four skills form the very basics of active listening. Over time, your child will develop and specialize in these skills. They may even put their own spin on these abilities to more accurately reflect their own way of emotional expression and comprehension. However much they may change later in life, these fundamentals will help get the ball rolling.

Obstacles

Unfortunately, very few things tied to the development of EI will ever be easy. Active listening is no exception, and there are a number of difficulties our children may encounter as they develop their listening skills. It is imperative that we know what these obstacles are so that we can be on the lookout for them and step in when we see our children struggling. It's worth noting that some obstacles tied to active listening are relatively straightforward and can be worked through easily. Others are tied more closely to disposition and cognition. In these instances, you may have to construct a holistic understanding of your child's personhood so you can know which solutions will work for them.

A Lack of Interest

This particular obstacle may present itself at the very beginning of the learning process. In those years when your child is still working to understand that others have emotions and that these emotions are important, they may fail to develop an interest in others' experiences. If they are continually motivated to pursue the acquisition of emotional skills, this obstacle should fall away. If not, consider taking steps to make your child more invested in improving their grasp of EI and its facets.

A Lack of Comprehension

Emotions are difficult to understand, especially for younger children. We have already explored the progression of emotional comprehension as it develops throughout your child's life. When they first begin to practice active listening, they may find it difficult to understand which skills to implement. However, the more they attempt to engage in active listening, the easier they will find it and the better they will understand what it entails. Along with this, time will teach your child how to receive communication and what to do with its message.

Difficulty Maintaining Focus

This obstacle results either from a child's difficulty following the speaker's train of thought or from a lack of mindful engagement. In the case of the latter, if your child is not fully engaged in the moment, their focus will be easily diverted by both external and internal stimuli. In the case of the former, difficulty following the conversation will result in your child only picking up bits and pieces. Their brain will then try to put together the entire puzzle based on these two pieces, which may not even be connected. Consequently, they will not receive the intended message.

Daydreams

This particular obstacle goes hand-in-hand with the inability to focus. If your child can't fully focus on the conversation, their mind may begin to wander. When this happens, it is only natural for your child's mind to slip into an imaginative state. In general, daydreaming is an excellent creative exercise. However, within the context of active listening, all it does is divert your child's attention from the speaker.

Interruptions

Interruptions can come from external sources, particularly if the conversation takes place in a busy or communal space. However, more often than not, your child will be the one interrupting their own active listening efforts. An important part of this practice is allowing the speaker the time and space to get their point across. You have to do so without interruption. Constant fidgeting, wandering eyes, moving about, or interjecting are all counterintuitive to the practice of active listening.

Emotional Obstacles

Internal obstacles often manifest as feelings of insecurity, doubt, and fear. These emotions may crop up due to the complex nature of a practice such as active listening. The more it requires your child to step outside of their emotional comfort zone, the more frequently they will experience these hindering feelings. This may persist if they do not immediately succeed at listening actively, and they may become discouraged. If this happens, it's time for motivation to make an appearance in the learning process.

Physical Obstacles

External obstacles can present themselves physically as anything from loud noises to bright, distracting visuals. If there are a large number of people present in the space where the conversation takes place, active listening will become all the more difficult. While it will not be impossible to push through physical obstacles, they will hinder effective communication on the part of the speaker as well as effective interpretation and response on the part of the listener.

How to Teach Active Listening

There are a number of techniques you can use to help your child develop their active listening skills. Later in this chapter, we will explore some general active listening activities. Before we get there, we must first expand upon the skills we have already taught our children. Combine these with the techniques outlined below, and your child will be well on their way to mastering this means of communication. Teach your child active listening by doing the following:

- Placing emphasis on eye contact. Teach your child to maintain eye contact during conversations. Not only does this help them concentrate on what is being said, but it will also let the speaker know that your child is paying attention, which will make the interaction all the more profound.

- Encouraging questions. Children show their investment in conversations through questions and supplement their comprehension of their contents with the answers provided. To facilitate this, you can read articles or excerpts from a book to your child and show them how to ask follow-up questions.

- Making learning fun through the use of listening games. Examples include asking your child to close their eyes while you play or make a sound and having them identify the noise, as well as a game in which you describe an object or scene while your child listens to and draws what you say.

- Helping them avoid interruptions. Teach your child why it is important to allow others to say their piece. Explain that this is vital, even if your child has a question or comment. Help them come up with ways to deal with this so they can concentrate during the conversation and remember what they wanted to say once the other person has finished speaking.

- Communicating clearly and effectively. You can do this first and foremost by modeling active listening for your child during conversations with them. However, you can also show them how the other end of communication works by speaking clearly and with intention. Give them instructions they can understand, and make sure your point comes across during conversation.

Tips for Active Listening

Teaching your child to become an active listener can be quite daunting. Given that this practice requires some effort and refinement, it may prove difficult for our children to adopt it easily. Fortunately, there are some general tips we can give them to make them better listeners.

Listen Face-to-Face

Face the person speaking to you and maintain eye contact as much as you can. Not only does this improve concentration, but it also shows respect and care on the part of the listener. Face-to-face communication is key, as the speaker may become distracted if they perceive the listener's gaze, and subsequently their attention, to be drifting.

Know When to Limit Aspects of Active Listening

Don't overdo the attention. Active listening is important for communication but must not be enforced too rigidly. That is to say; your child should use their listening skills naturally during conversations. Don't stare unblinkingly at the speaker, as this may prove just as distracting. Moreover, don't become overly invested in the other person's emotional experience. Tune into the conversation and listen actively, but do so within reason.

Avoid Interruptions at All Costs

Try not to interrupt. Sometimes, this may be unavoidable. However, for the most part, questions and comments can wait until the conclusion of the speaker's turn. Without interruptions, conversations will flow more easily, and communication will take place effectively.

Keep Questions Pertinent

Ask questions that are to the point. If a conversation is wide-ranging or long, your child may feel the impulse or need to ask just as many questions in order to address every single aspect. Keep communication clear and effective by identifying the most important aspects of the conversation and asking insightful questions that focus on their comprehension or expansion.

Embrace Empathy as You Listen

Integrate other aspects of EI. When you listen actively, you are trying to make the other person feel seen and heard. Another effective way of doing this is through the demonstration of empathy. Teach your child to empathize when listening to the people in their life. Not only will this make the speaker feel understood, but it will also enhance the relationship between them and your child.

Being a Good Role Model

Time and time again, we have revisited the importance of behavioral modeling for the purpose of building EI. When it comes to active listening, one of the best ways for us to teach our children is to show them what a good listener looks like. However, it can also be difficult for us to know if we are being good role models. While it is easy to read theory concerning the traits and behaviors of good listeners, we might not always be sure if we are demonstrating the same things in our own lives. To ensure that you are modeling positive listening behaviors, ask yourself the following questions (and answer them honestly):

- When my child is speaking to me, am I distraction-free, or is there something that takes my attention away from them?

- When listening, do I make sure to look my child in the eyes?

- Does my mind wander during conversations with my child, or do I keep my mind focused on what they are telling me?

- Are my responses appropriate, i.e., am I asking insightful follow-up questions and giving them nonverbal cues to encourage continued discussion?

Active Listening Activities

With our understanding of active listening as a concept now firmly in place, the time has once again come for us to see how we can teach and reinforce this knowledge practically. As with the preceding chapters, read through each of the activities below and take note of those you believe to be most suited to your child. If you think that some activities might work for your child but that they don't entirely line up with their learning style or interests, feel free to adjust the particulars to make them work for your child. Activities to support active listening include:

- Simon says.

- The telephone game, in which a piece of information is passed from person to person with the aim of making it down the line intact.

- Giving your child detailed directions and instructions, for instance, as part of a scavenger hunt.

- Involving your child in cooking, and reading the recipe to them so that they may execute the steps.

- Freeze dancing or a round of musical statues.

- Red light, green light.

- Spot the Change, in which you start with certain words or sounds and subtly change them each round. Ask your child to identify the new word or sound as well as describe what has changed.

- Constructing a sound scavenger hunt (think something akin to "Marco Polo"). Add a layer of complexity to this activity by asking your child to take note of all the things they hear throughout the hunt and to report them back once the game is finished.

Honing Your Child's Communication Skills

Now that we have mastered one side of the communication equation, we can move on to the other. In addition to being good listeners, our children must know how to communicate their needs and experiences. Help them build on both areas of expertise by doing the following:

- Regularly engage in conversations with your child. By doing this, you become an example for your child, demonstrating what good communication looks like. As you converse, remember to do so with intention. Though your goal is to have your child be a better communicator, make sure your discussion also has a point. Remember that conversations require multiple inputs, and allow your child to provide an opinion or comment on what you say.

- Describe your experiences throughout the day. Once again, you teach through example. When you sit down for dinner with your child, talk about how your day went. Illustrate your actions, thoughts, and emotions. Encourage reciprocity by asking your child about their day as well and seeking details of commensurate value to those you have provided.

- Construct learning opportunities. If your child has difficulty communicating, take some time to practice mock conversations with them. Choose a topic and help them flesh out the details. Practice the give-and-take of communication by allowing them to ask questions as well as answering any queries from your side. These exercises are doubly effective as your child practices their listening and expression skills simultaneously.

- Listen and repeat what your child shares with you. Teach them how to take information and expand upon it within the context of conversations. An easy way to do this is to take a statement they have made, partially repeat it, and then tack on a conclusion or question. This will allow your child to expand upon their original point, perhaps say something new, and keep the conversation rolling.

- Help your child understand nonverbal cues. Either through demonstration or by using examples, help your child practice the identification and analysis of body language.

- Strike up a conversation with your child with the express purpose of having some fun. Learning doesn't have to be boring or clinical. By providing your child with some fun conversational prompts (for example, "What do you think the ice at the North Pole tastes like?), you provide them with an opportunity to use their imagination. If you ask them something more personal, they will have the chance to talk about something they like. This will demonstrate your child's ability to speak passionately, which you can help them use more during communication.

- Use literature as an entry point for discussion. Take time as often as you can to read something with your child. Start off by reading entire chapters or books yourself. When your child is ready, ask them to read sections by themselves or to help you complete sentences. Once you have finished the book, have a discussion about the plot, characters, themes, and anything else that stood out to either of you. By using this shared experience as a conversation starter, your child treads familiar ground when communicating and can build up their confidence.

- Get physical, like a game of conversational catch. This is exactly what it sounds like. Take a ball and play a game of catch with the added rule that every throw has to be accompanied by an answer or a question.

- Encourage your child to be opinionated. During discussions, ask for your child's feedback and perspective, especially regarding topics that have an effect on their lives. In doing so, you enable them to reflect on their experiences and emotions. This leads to better self-awareness and expression, both of which contribute to more effective communication.

- Introduce reflection by means of journaling. You may find that your child communicates more clearly and healthily if they first examine their experiences and the emotions they elicit. Working through emotions through journaling can help your child figure out what it is they want to communicate and may even enable them to determine how they want to structure this communication.

Teaching Your Child How to Self-Advocate

If we hope to help our children become effective, healthy communicators, we must help them develop the skills and confidence to stand up for and express themselves. This can manifest in many different ways, depending on your child's temperament and general disposition. However, for us as parents, this means teaching our children self-advocacy.

Being able to advocate for yourself is an essential part of communication, and self-advocacy involves doing just that. The practice involves building a skillset that enables your child to communicate their needs, desires, interests, and rights. In addition to simply communicating these things, self-advocacy involves the ability to negotiate and be assertive. Having these skills comes with the obligation to make considered, informed decisions and to hold yourself accountable for any decisions made (Lee, 2019).

By studying the definition alone, we can already see why self-advocacy is such an important part of communicating at any age. Fortunately, the benefits of this practice stretch even further, as its cultivation provides children with feelings of safety and comfort, especially with regards to their own personhood. Additionally, self-advocacy has been tied to higher levels of achievement and happiness in formal environments such as school and work (Lee, 2019). These elevations are largely linked to the self-confidence that self-advocacy affords practitioners, given that they will feel more secure in their decisions and will know how to navigate the difficulties of life.

Perhaps most importantly of all, self-advocacy ties in nicely with two of the fundamental aspects of EI, namely self-awareness and self-regulation. The practice involves knowing what your needs are and how they can be best expressed. With regards to self-regulation, someone who advocates for themselves will also know how to manage and modulate their feelings and behaviors in order to move through difficulties and see that their needs are fully met. By adopting this one practice, we empower our children to improve two distinct, essential pillars of their emotional intelligence.

Teaching Self-Regulation

Helping your child become their own advocate starts with teaching them to gain and maintain control over as much of their personhood as they can. There are a number of different ways in which you can facilitate the development of self-regulation. As always, use this information as a framework to build your own approach. The more personalized your techniques are, the more profoundly they will resonate with your child.

Don't Wait Too Long

Helping your child develop emotional and social skills can never be done too early. We know that children possess an awareness of emotions from a very early age. Teaching them to take control of these experiences will help them as they grow up and encounter more emotionally complex situations. Starting early is proactive and will help your child understand the importance of self-regulation and self-advocacy.

Facilitate Self-Awareness

The older your children become, the more aware they will be of all the different aspects of their personalities. Encouraging them to be self-aware will also enable them to identify their limits, strengths, and weaknesses. With this understanding in place, they will know when to ask for help and how much assistance they need. The best way for you to facilitate this is through practice. Construct scenarios in which they can use their self-awareness skills to ask for help as well as work through moments of difficulty.

Along with these more cerebral activities, remember to help your child develop physical self-awareness. Teach them to listen to what their body is telling them, as well as to respond to these biological messages. In doing so, they learn how to self-regulate and how to communicate what they need to fulfill their physical needs.

Allow Them to Take Ownership of Their Problems

Though your instinct might be to take your kids' problems off their hands, the best way for them to gain the skills they need is to allow them to work through them themselves. This does not mean that you should be entirely hands-off. Instead, ask them about their issues, listen actively as they talk about them, and validate their feelings. If you do want to help out, don't intervene beyond helping them brainstorm some solutions to their problem.

Allow Them to Take Ownership of Their Feelings

In order to express what they need, children first need to understand what they are feeling. Through this comprehension, they can also determine how they need to communicate these emotions in a healthy, appropriate manner. To facilitate ownership, don't label your child's emotions for them. Help them define themselves and determine what the best means of expression will be.

Remain Positive

Learning to self-regulate and self-advocate may be a difficult process. Even though humans are innately emotional creatures, working with these emotions may not come naturally to everyone. When your child falters or fails, be there to support them. Let them know that you are proud of their efforts, and reassure them that they can learn from their mistakes. Keep the faith, and your child will eventually find the approach to regulation and advocacy that works for them.

Facilitate and Encourage Critical Thinking

Your child will need to make decisions regarding communication and emotional regulation at some point. In order to find constructive and appropriate ways to do this, they will need to think critically. Help them suss out their approach and technique by providing them with a low-stakes, calm environment in which to hone their cognitive skills. This space will help them build self-confidence as well as improve their awareness of what they are capable of. You can help them along by asking leading questions such as "Do you think that option A is better than option B in this specific context?" or "When you are confronted with these feelings or events, what happens in your head, and what can you do to make things better?"

Facilitate and Encourage Solving Problems

Similar to letting them take ownership of their problems, help them solve these issues without taking over entirely. Your child needs to build confidence in their problem-solving skills as well as become aware of the extent of these abilities. When they tell you about a problem, hear them out and help them figure out a way forward. Allow them to implement these strategies on their own. If they don't work out, allow your child to amend their approach themselves. This will build their skills and help them in the face of adversity down the line.

Instill Independence

Your child will learn to advocate for themselves the more they can assert their independence and have the chance to do things their way. You can provide your child with these opportunities by having them ask for assistance in a store or at school without your help. Start off with small practices and build up their independence until they feel confident and able to speak up for themselves without prompting or help.

Get Them Involved

This method is all about empowering your child to make their own decisions. By giving them control over decisions, you teach them how to handle power, how to be responsible, and how to compromise. Start small with everyday decisions such as clothing for the school day or a snack for lunch. Over time, you can increase the scale of these decisions so that they may gradually learn to exert more control over their lives.

Plan Ahead

Your child will go through many changes in life. By involving them in the process, you not only prepare them to handle transitions better but also teach them how to take control of things affecting their lives. When your child has a big transition coming up, say from one school year to the next, ask them how they will handle it and help them brainstorm the best way to communicate what they need in this new time, as well as the steps they will take to get what they need from the experience.

Build Their Self-Esteem

The more confident your child is in themselves, the more effective their communication will be and the more in control they will feel over their life. The simplest way to build up self-esteem is through praise. When your child succeeds in communicating or managing their emotions, acknowledge this and praise their achievement. Even if they fail, tell them you are proud of them for trying and remind them that they can do all they set their mind to.

Encourage Wide-Ranging Communication

Exposing your child to a wide variety of situations that require communication will teach them how to regulate and manage this skill in different contexts. You can start this practice at home by acting out hypothetical situations. When your child is ready, have them apply their skills and knowledge in the real world. Encourage them to speak to their doctors directly during their next check-up or to respond in a friendly way when greeted by a cashier. You can also teach your child more than just how to speak to older people. Help build their communication skills by practicing situations in which a specific emotion is present. Act out scenarios in which they feel angry, threatened, or uncomfortable to teach them how to handle and diffuse these situations.

Emphasize the Importance of Self-Advocacy

Your child may be afraid to speak up for themselves because they fear offending others or stirring up trouble. When this happens, remind them of the importance of self-advocacy. Use yourself as an example, and tell them of a time when you advocated for yourself, and it yielded successful results. Teach them that while speaking up won't take away issues immediately or completely; it can make their lives a whole lot easier and safer.

Tips for Self-Advocacy

The process of teaching your child self-advocacy may prove difficult, especially if your child is more reserved or if they cling to restrictive ideas of propriety and self-regulation. To help make things easier for both yourself and your child, you can do the following:

- Help your child determine where their strengths lie and focus on building their communication skills around these abilities.

- Allow your child to make their own decisions regarding their needs and how to make sure that they achieve their desired results. This fosters independence and teaches your child certain aspects of self-advocacy in a safe, controlled environment.

- Reassure your child that their journey is not solitary and that they will have your support and guidance throughout.

Supporting Self-Advocacy in the Home

Your home is one of the first environments in which your child will learn many of their emotional skills. Fortunately, you have the ability to control the nature of the environment and make it conducive to the development of abilities such as self-advocacy. Supporting your child as they learn to speak up for themselves can be very easy, and these supportive measures include:

- Encourage your child to explore the world around them as well as their place in it. Through self-exploration, your child will gain self-awareness, and know where and when they need to speak up.

- Reassuring and reminding your child that they don't have to do everything alone and that they can ask you for help. Supplement their self-advocacy abilities by praising them for knowing to reach out.

- Let your child know what your own emotional needs and expectations are so that they can understand what they have to bring to the table. In doing so, they will also be encouraged to share these things with you in kind.

- Learning to say "yes" more often. This does not mean that you have to become entirely permissive, but you have to allow your child a bit more freedom. Crucially, you have to keep "no" in your back pocket to reinforce the boundaries you and your child have set.

- Listening to your child as opposed to jumping in and taking control. Allow them to talk through their problems and strategize solutions. Give feedback if prompted, or simply listen if your child wants to vent.

Validating their wishes and feelings will empower them to advocate for themselves more.

- Providing them with choices when helping them solve problems so that they can select the option that is most suited to their needs and sensibilities.

- Providing them with the space they need to express themselves and figure out what it is they want or need from you by way of support. In this space, they develop self-awareness and self-regulation. You don't have to go very far, but just give them enough space to find their own way while still feeling your support.

Conflict Resolution for Kids

The final component of healthy communication is having the ability to address and work through times of conflict. We have to teach conflict resolution to our children, as it is to be expected that they will butt heads with a few people (possibly ourselves included) throughout their lives. Knowing how to defuse and resolve conflict will help them live emotionally healthy lives as well as contribute positively to their interpersonal skills. Because conflict resolution is such a practical thing, we will explore how we can help our children learn this particular skill. Along the way, we ourselves may pick up a thing or two.

What to Do

The very first thing to do when teaching your child conflict resolution is to take a step back and calm down. Conflict elicits a lot of big, complex emotions. From experience, we know that when we feel overly emotional, the logical part of our brains tends to become cloudy and may not function as well. Have both yourself and your child take a step back, take a deep breath, and approach the situation from a place of peace and clarity.

Work Through Emotions Before Anything Else

Once you have taken that step and breathed, start the resolution process by helping your child understand exactly how the conflict is making them feel. Without doing it on their behalf, help your child label their emotions. By pinpointing the precise feelings that are characterizing that experience, your child will be able to more easily construct the road to resolution. Determining your child's emotions can be helped by using the following visual aids:

- A visual feelings chart that is made up of illustrated faces displaying different facial expressions.

- An emotional stoplight your child can use by pointing to the different colored lights. Red signifies emotions that are still too overwhelming for the resolution process to begin. Yellow denotes that they are starting to calm down but still need a minute to compose themselves. Green represents a state in which your child feels ready to deal with their feelings and tackle the issue.

- An emotion thermometer. Your child can point to the different numbers on the thermometer to indicate the intensity of their emotional state. The higher the number, the higher the intensity.

Discuss the Nature of the Conflict

With emotions labeled, you can start to look at the situation itself. Ask your child to describe their experience in as much detail as they can recall. Listen intently, and then help them get to the root of the cause. Understanding the event of origin will enable your child to solve the entire problem instead of simply addressing the topmost layers of the conflict. Additionally, this is a learning experience for your child, and they can use what they implement in this scenario to resolve future conflicts as well.

Determine a Positive Solution

The solution you and your child construct should contribute positively to their emotional development. Some strategies you can use to ensure that the resolution of the conflict is positive include:

- Problem-solving baseball, in which each base represents a stage of the conflict resolution process. The first base labels the problem, the second base presents possible actionable options, the third base selects the most positive option, and home base evaluates whether the decision was truly positive and conducive to your child's emotional development.

- Rating the solution using smiley faces. Ask your child whether the solution you have decided upon will improve their mood, worsen it, or not really affect it at all. Use smiley faces that demonstrate a sliding scale of happiness to help your child determine the efficacy of their decision.

Gain Some Perspective

Because conflicts are such big emotional experiences, they can overshadow everything in your child's life. It's important to gain perspective so that the conflict may not only be handled effectively but also in such a way that it will open up the way for your child to move on. They can do this by simply casting their mind over the entirety of their relationship with the person with whom they are in conflict. Your child must consider the importance and nature of this relationship and whether they wish to sacrifice it because of one hiccup.

Another effective method of gaining perspective is by empathizing. If your child is able to inhabit the point of view of the other person, they may be able to understand why the conflict originated and why it has progressed in the way it has. Finally, your child must consider other factors that may have influenced the experience that caused the conflict. They must consider the context in which it took place, more specifically, the events that led up to it, as well as whether your child's behavior may have contributed in any way.

Use Your Communication Skills

It is imperative that your child be able to express how the conflict makes them feel. In the context of conflict resolution, they must be able to do so without making things personal or resorting to insults and accusations. Your child can improve their communication in these situations by using "I" statements instead of "You" statements, which tend to lean towards finger-pointing.

Your child can also take a pen and a piece of paper and write down what they hope to communicate. This planning can make their communication more effective and may also help them refine what they would like to convey in the resolution process.

You can also lend a hand by doing some resolution-oriented roleplay. Have your child act out what they want to say to resolve the situation, and help them find the best way of getting their point across.

Agree, Respect, and Follow Up

You can help your child wrap up the conflict resolution process by contributing your opinion to their choice of solution. Help them ensure that their choice is positive and that it will be to the benefit of everyone involved. If you don't agree with their decision, be sure to remain respectful of it and to recognize their autonomy in this decision-making process. Finally, you have to follow up to see if your child followed through. This is especially important if your child is the guilty party, but it must also be done if they can be considered the victim in the situation. Following up means checking in to see if your child enacted their solution and whether it proved effective. If it didn't quite work out for them, help your child brainstorm a new plan, and similarly, check in soon after you have decided on the improved solution.

What Not to Do

Name-Calling

Discourage your child from calling other children names, as this may worsen the conflict and result in your child making matters much more personally incisive than they ought to be.

Getting Physical

At no point should your child engage in physical violence. Not only can this cause genuine injury and bodily harm, but it also negates everything that characterizes dealing with life's issues in an emotionally intelligent way.

Interrupting

If there are certain things your child wishes to say about the conflict to the other person involved, they must allow the latter to do the same. Conflict resolution involves the use of active listening skills, which we know include your child allowing another to speak without interruption. Letting the other person express their own feelings before speaking will make the resolution process easier, as frequent interjections may make them feel as though your child is not listening or does not care what they have to say.

Refusing to Listen

Resolving conflict involves communication, a large part of which involves listening. Similar to your child's need to express their feelings regarding the conflict, the other person involved in the matter should also be allowed to say their piece. By refusing to listen, your child is not being emotionally intelligent. Instead, this refusal is tantamount to the invalidation of the other person's feelings and will prevent a positive resolution from taking place.

Resorting to Insults

This refers specifically to insulting another child's intelligence. In the same way that name-calling may make matters worse, resorting to insults reflects badly on your child. It suggests a sense of superiority and may very well shut down any and all opportunities for conflict resolution.

Using the Hand Technique to Resolve Conflict

The hand technique is a quick and excellent way to gain an understanding of the conflict as well as present and select an actionable solution. This method involves the entire hand, as each finger has a prompt that signifies a part of the resolution process. Have your child hold up their hand and respond to each of your prompts using the designated finger or fingers.

Start with the thumb, and ask your child to state what the problem is. If possible, have them state the issue that lies at the very root of the situation. Next, use the index, middle, and ring fingers to list three separate solutions. Finally, use the pinky to make a decision and select the most positive, healthiest solution.

Conflict Resolution Activities

In addition to the do's and don'ts that can help us shape our approach to conflict resolution, there are a number of activities we can use to simplify the process and make it more relatable for our children.

Resolution Worksheets

There are a number of conflict resolution worksheets available for download from the Internet. These worksheets can help your child identify their approach to conflict resolution as well as map out their approach to dealing with the situation. Some of these worksheets will also enable your child to understand

and write down their feelings regarding the situation. In doing so, they commit a plan to paper, one that will help them see the conflict through and mend the fences that need mending.

Roleplay

This activity can center around the specific conflict your child is experiencing or be used for general practice. On pieces of paper, write down different scenarios in which your child may encounter adversity or conflict. Have you and your child assume the roles of the offender and victim in turn and act out the resolution process. Once finished, discuss the scenarios and the ways in which you chose to deal with them.

Comparing the Scale of the Conflict

This activity can also be done using a worksheet or through simple discussion. Sit down with your child and have them compare the current conflicts they are facing. Then, have them reflect on similar difficulties they have experienced in the past. Ask your child to consider how they handled these previous conflicts, more specifically, whether they could resolve them on their own or needed to ask you for help. Next, ask them to consider whether their present problem is bigger or smaller than the one from before. If it is bigger, then you can help your child resolve the conflict. If it is smaller, you can help them in some measure, but you must encourage them to take initiative and do the bulk of the emotional work themselves.

Writing Prompts

Give your child a prompt such as "If my friend did [insert unconscionable action here] to me, I would fight them immediately." Have your child write down what exactly they would do as well as why they would feel moved to take this particular action. Once done, ask them to read it back to you. Discuss what they have written and whether they feel the action warrants their chosen response. If they say yes, explain to them why that may not be the case and help them find another approach. If they say no, congratulate them on their reasoning and ask them if they can find another way to resolve the situation. In this case, allow them to take charge, but provide your help when needed.

Games

There are a number of different games you can play with your child to teach them how to handle conflicts. Many of these games are available online. However, there is a game that you can put together using a more DIY approach. As a variation on charades, you write down several conflict scenarios on some pieces of paper. In addition to this, write down categories into which the solution must fall, ranging from "me" to an entire friend group or family. Taking it in turns, select a scenario and a category and construct a solution on the fly. If you'd like, you can time the rounds and discuss the solutions after each one. The more you and your child play this game, the quicker they will theorize solutions and the more sophisticated their suggestions will become.

With conflict resolution taught to our children, we have slotted the very last tool into our child's emotional utility belt. Once they have mastered this, or at the very least gotten the hang of it, they are on their way to living an emotionally enriched life. Though they may not always solve conflicts on their first try, they will understand the need for a second attempt and will do their best to ensure that the friction in their relationships soon turns to harmony.

Conclusion

And so, our journey together comes to an end. Now you can take a look at all you have learned and feel proud of the progress you have made. When you started this book, you were just beginning to understand what emotional intelligence is and how it measures up against more traditional academic prowess. From there, you learned how to determine your parenting style, how to make your child emotionally literate, how to instill a growth mindset, teach them self-awareness and self-advocacy, and even help them become better communicators. Perhaps most impressive of all, you learned how to be an emotionally intelligent parent yourself. You've come a long way since we met one another in the introduction. As much praise as you heap on your child, you can feel just as proud of how much progress has been made in your own life.

From here, the real work begins as you and your child learn what it means to live an emotionally intelligent life. For some of you, this may be exciting, while others will be nervous about the road ahead. Rest assured that for all of you, the journey will be interesting, and you will be glad you took it once you reach the other side. You have accepted this undertaking because you want the best for your child, and EI has never been more important than it is now. Draw on all you have learned within the pages of this book and incorporate it into your parenting approach. In doing so, you will empower your children to face life's peaks and valleys with a strength they never knew they could possess. Once they have come to the end of their own journey, your child will be the best version of themselves they could ever hope to be.

My hope is that you will walk away from this book with an appreciation for all that you are capable of. If you feel this book has changed or empowered you in some way, why not pay it forward by helping others change their own children's lives for the better? Consider writing us a review after your purchase, or maybe even buying this book for another parent in your life. Who knows? Maybe the both of you will someday be the parents of the emotionally intelligent kids who changed the world. In fairness, success on a smaller scale is more likely, but then again, it's natural for us parents to dream.

References

Ackerman, C. (2019, April 28). *Goal setting for students, kids, & teens (Incl. worksheets & templates)*. PositivePsychology.com. https://positivepsychology.com/goal-setting-students-kids/

Adamovic, B. (2014, September 3). *Good parenting - How to control emotions and be a calm parent*. Kids First Community. https://www.kidsfirstcommunity.com/good-parenting-how-to-control-emotions-and-be-a-calm-parent/

American Academy of Pediatrics. (2019). *How to understand your child's temperament*. HealthyChildren.org. https://www.healthychildren.org/English/ages-stages/gradeschool/Pages/How-to-Understand-Your-Childs-Temperament.aspx

Asztalos, R. (2020, May 20). *How to respond when children cry*. Encouraging Discipline. https://encouragingdiscipline.com/how-to-respond-when-children-cry/

Autuori-Dedic, J. (2023, June 8). *4 big emotions to be sure you're talking about with little kids*. Parents. https://www.parents.com/toddlers-preschoolers/development/intellectual/list-of-emotions-to-talk-about-with-kids/

Bayless, K. (2022, October 12). *Helicopter parenting and 5 ways it impacts kids*. Parents. https://www.parents.com/parenting/better-

parenting/what-is-helicopter-
parenting/#:~:text=be%20a%20problem%3F-

BetterHelp Editorial Team. (2023, May 10). *What is gentle
parenting and should I integrate it into my family's life?*
BetterHelp.
https://www.betterhelp.com/advice/parenting/what-
is-gentle-parenting/

Blackard, B. (2013, July). *Why I let kids cry.* Language of
Listening.   https://www.languageoflistening.com/let-
kids-cry/

Borelli, J. L., & Lai, J. (2019, June 25). *How to decipher the emotions
behind   your   child's   behaviors.*   Greater   Good.
https://greatergood.berkeley.edu/article/item/how_to
_decipher_the_emotions_behind_your_childs_behavior
s

Bracken, A. (2022, September 4). *7 values to teach your child by age
10.*   Parents.
https://www.parents.com/parenting/better-
parenting/values-to-teach-your-child-by-age-10/

Brady, K. (2019, December 4). *How to cope with different parenting
styles.*   Keir   Brady   Counseling   Services.
https://keirbradycounseling.com/parenting-styles/

Brandwein, S. (2022, February 4). *The importance of self-regulation
and   how   to   teach   it   to   your   kids.*   Moshi.
https://www.moshikids.com/articles/how-to-teach-
self-regulation-to-kids/

Breault, R. (n.d.). *Robert Breault quote: "A child seldom needs a good
talking   to   as   a   good   listening   to."*   QuoteFancy.
https://quotefancy.com/quote/1579257/Robert-
Breault-A-child-seldom-needs-a-good-talking-to-as-a-
good-listening-to

Briggs, R. D. (2023, January 12). *Positive parenting: Discipline vs. punishment.* Psychology Today. https://www.psychologytoday.com/intl/blog/on-babies/202301/discipline-vs-punishment

Brody, B. (2021, February 25). *What are the different parenting styles?* WebMD. https://www.webmd.com/parenting/features/parenting-styles

Canfield, J. (2007). *How to get from where you are to where you want to be: The 25 principles of success.* Harper Collins Publishers.

Canfield, J. (2013). *Chicken soup for the soul 20th anniversary edition.* Simon and Schuster.

CBT for kids: Thoughts, feelings, & actions (worksheet). (2012). Therapist Aid. https://www.therapistaid.com/therapy-worksheet/cbt-for-kids/cbt/children

Chancellor, J. (2008, February 24). *Why emotional intelligence (EQ) is more important than IQ.* Owlcation. https://owlcation.com/social-sciences/Why-Emotional-Intelligence-is-More-Important-Than-IQ

Cherry, K. (2013, October 11). *IQ vs. EQ: Which one is more important?* Verywell Mind. https://www.verywellmind.com/iq-or-eq-which-one-is-more-important-2795287

Cherry, K. (2022a, January 26). *5 key components of emotional intelligence.* Verywell Mind. https://www.verywellmind.com/components-of-emotional-intelligence-2795438

Cherry, K. (2022b, November 7). *What is emotional intelligence?* Verywell Mind. https://www.verywellmind.com/what-is-emotional-intelligence-2795423

Children's learning styles. (2020, September 3). AbilityPath. https://abilitypath.org/ap-resources/childrens-learning-styles/#:~:text=The%20best%20way%20to%20learn

Cinelli, E. (2023, May 27). *Discover your child's learning style: A guide for parents.* Parents. https://www.parents.com/discover-your-childs-learning-style-7368094

Connors, H. (2019, February 13). *How to teach SMART goal setting for kids | Free goal setting worksheet.* Simplify Create Inspire. https://www.simplifycreateinspire.com/goal-setting-for-kids/

Conway, S. (2021, April 15). *5 opportunities for teaching empathy in everyday life.* Mother Duck Child Care. https://www.motherduck.com.au/5-opportunities-for-teaching-empathy-in-every-day-life/

Cornwall, G. (2022, April 14). *How to instill a "growth mindset" in kids.* U.S. News. https://www.usnews.com/education/k12/articles/how-to-instill-a-growth-mindset-in-kids

Craycroft, M. (2019, October 4). *Teaching children emotional intelligence.* Carrots Are Orange. https://carrotsareorange.com/teaching-children-emotional-intelligence/

Crockett, L. (2019, June 26). *10 of the best growth mindset activities for kids.* Future Focused Learning. https://blog.futurefocusedlearning.net/growth-mindset-activities-kids

Crowe, A. (2022a, April 21). *10 educational goal examples to keep kids motivated.* Prodigy.

https://www.prodigygame.com/main-en/blog/educational-goals/

Crowe, A. (2022b, June 20). *27 positive affirmations for kids (and parents!).* Prodigy. https://www.prodigygame.com/main-en/blog/positive-affirmations-for-kids/#:~:text=Positive%20affirmations%20for%20kids%20about

Cullins, A. (2019a, January 4). *7 fun goal-setting activities for children.* Big Life Journal. https://biglifejournal.com/blogs/blog/5-fun-goal-setting-activities-children

Cullins, A. (2019b, October 22). *Key strategies to teach children empathy (sorted by age).* Big Life Journal. https://biglifejournal.com/blogs/blog/key-strategies-teach-children-empathy

Dajczak, A. (2021, February 23). *How to identify your child's learning style.* PA Virtual Charter School. https://blog.pavcsk12.org/how-to-identify-your-childs-learning-style

Davis, A. (2021, December 7). *Partners with different parenting styles: How to make it work.* Adventures from Scratch. https://www.adventurebook.com/connect/different-parenting-styles/

Developing listening skills for kids. (2022, May 29). Listenwise. https://listenwise.com/developing-listening-skills-for-kids/

Dewar, G. (2015, January 21). *Empathy and kindness: Early developmental milestones.* The Urban Child Institute. http://www.urbanchildinstitute.org/articles/features/empathy-and-kindness-early-developmental-milestones

Dewar, G. (2017, July 2). *The authoritative parenting style: An evidence-based guide.* Parenting Science. https://parentingscience.com/authoritative-parenting-style/

Dewar, G. (2018, August 2). *The authoritarian parenting style: What does it look like?* Parenting Science. https://parentingscience.com/authoritarian-parenting-style/

Dewar, G. (2019, September 2). *Permissive parenting: An evidence-based guide.* Parenting Science. https://parentingscience.com/permissive-parenting/

Dewar, G. (2020, August 22). *Teaching empathy: Evidence-based tips for fostering empathic awareness in children.* Parenting Science. https://parentingscience.com/teaching-empathy-tips/

Dodge, A. (2019, August 27). *Why emotional intelligence is the hardest but most important lesson.* Ozobot. https://ozobot.com/why-emotional-intelligence-is-the-hardest-but-most-important-lesson/

Doyle Bryant, C. (2022). *What is empathy? Definition for kids.* Talking with Trees. https://talkingtreebooks.com/teaching-resources-catalog/definitions/what-is-empathy.html

Dweck, C. (2015, March 2). *Carol Dweck: A summary of the two mindsets.* Farnam Street. https://fs.blog/carol-dweck-mindset/

Dweck, C. (2016, January 13). *What having a "growth mindset" actually means.* Harvard Business Review. https://hbr.org/2016/01/what-having-a-growth-mindset-actually-means

Dweck, C. S. (2006). *Mindset: The new psychology of success.* Random House.

Early signs of emotional intelligence in toddlers. (2020, June 9). BabySparks. https://babysparks.com/2020/06/09/early-signs-of-emotional-intelligence-in-toddlers/

Emotional intelligence. (2019). Psychology Today. https://www.psychologytoday.com/intl/basics/emotional-intelligence

Encouraging children to name their emotions. (2017, March 27). Goodstart Early Learning. https://www.goodstart.org.au/parenting/encouraging-children-to-name-their-emotions#:~:text=The%20first%20step%20is%20to

Engler, B. (2021, October 12). *Building conflict resolution skills in children.* Connections Academy. https://www.connectionsacademy.com/support/resources/article/building-conflict-resolution-skills-in-children/

EQ vs IQ - Difference and comparison. (2019). Diffen. https://www.diffen.com/difference/EQ_vs_IQ

Farnsworth Finn, J. (2020, February 1). *Pre-K self-awareness tips: Here's how to help your child.* Today. https://www.today.com/parenting-guides/pre-kindergarten-self-awareness-tips-t177473

Ferriss, T. (2021, February 18). *Tim Ferriss quote: "Kids don't do what you say. They do what they see. How you live your life is their example."* QuoteFancy. https://quotefancy.com/quote/2516914/Tim-Ferriss-Kids-don-t-do-what-you-say-They-do-what-they-see-How-you-live-your-life-is

Firestone, L. (2016, March 17). *Why we need to teach kids emotional intelligence.* PsychAlive. https://www.psychalive.org/why-we-need-to-teach-kids-emotional-intelligence/

4 benefits of teaching emotional intelligence during early childhood. (2020, December 10). Cornerstone Learning Center. https://learnatcornerstone.com/teaching-emotional-intelligence/

5 ways to teach your child active listening skills. (2020, October 7). The Gardner School. https://www.thegardnerschool.com/blog/5-ways-to-teach-your-child-active-listening-skills/

Garey, J. (2023, March 28). *Teaching kids how to deal with conflict.* Child Mind Institute. https://childmind.org/article/teaching-kids-how-to-deal-with-conflict/

Gibran, K. (2002). The prophet. Prophet.

Gilles, G. (2015, January 7). *How to be an emotionally intelligent parent - Part I.* MentalHelp.net. https://www.mentalhelp.net/blogs/how-to-be-an-emotionally-intelligent-parent-part-i/

Ginsburg, K. R., & Moraghan Jablow, M. (2015). *Building resilience in children and teens: Giving kids roots and wings.* American Academy Of Pediatrics.

Glista, D. (2021, September 29). *How to identify your child's learning style.* Scholars Education. https://www.scholarsed.com/child-learning-style/

Goggins, D. (2019). *Can't hurt me: Master your mind and defy the odds.* Lioncrest Publishing, Druk.

Goh, J. (2017, March 7). *5 ways to help children identify and express their emotions.* MindChamps. https://www.mindchamps.org/blog/help-children-identify-express-emotions/

Gold, C. M. (2014, May 22). *11 tips to understand emotional development in children.* MomJunction. https://www.momjunction.com/articles/helpful-tips-understand-child-psychology_0074385/

Goleman, D. (1995). *Emotional intelligence: Why it can matter more than IQ.* Bloomsbury.

Golis, C. (2017). *History of EQ - Emotional intelligence.* Practical Emotional Intelligence. https://www.emotionalintelligencecourse.com/history-of-eq/

Gongala, S. (2015, June 29). *Tips on how to improve your child's self-awareness?* MomJunction. https://www.momjunction.com/articles/teach-self-awareness-to-your-child_00359060/

Gregory, L. (2023, March 17). *Conflict resolution activities for children.* Brightwheel. https://mybrightwheel.com/blog/conflict-resolution-activities-for-kids

Grossman, A. L. (2021a, January 6). *Goal setting for kids (How to explain goals to a child).* Money Prodigy. https://www.moneyprodigy.com/goal-setting-for-kids/

Grossman, A. L. (2021b, February 5). *Short term goals for kids (37 list example ideas).* Money Prodigy. https://www.moneyprodigy.com/short-term-goals-for-kids/

Hart, L. (2019). *Parenting quotes on discipline: On loving unconditionally.* Positive Parenting Ally. https://www.positive-parenting-ally.com/quotes-on-discipline.html

Harvard Graduate School of Education. (2018, October 13). *5 tips for cultivating empathy.* Making Caring Common. https://mcc.gse.harvard.edu/resources-for-families/5-tips-cultivating-empathy

Help your child explore their natural talents. (2022, January 14). The Gardner School. https://www.thegardnerschool.com/blog/ways-to-help-your-child-explore-their-natural-talents/

Higuera, V. (2019a, September 12). *What is helicopter parenting?* Healthline. https://www.healthline.com/health/parenting/helicopter-parenting

Higuera, V. (2019b, September 20). *What is uninvolved parenting?* Healthline. https://www.healthline.com/health/parenting/uninvolved-parenting

Howard, L. (2020, April 29). *Why is empathy important for kids? Tips to build empathy in children.* Atlanta Innovative Counseling Center. https://www.atlantainnovativecounseling.com/aicc-blog/why-is-empathy-important-for-kids-tips-to-build-empathy-in-children#:~:text=Experts%20agree%20that%20empathy%20is

Huerta, D. (2018, November 7). *Perseverance: How your kids can overcome hardship.* Focus on the Family. https://www.focusonthefamily.com/parenting/perseverance-how-your-kids-can-overcome-hardship/

Improve your child's active listening skills. (2017, July 27). Oxford Learning. https://www.oxfordlearning.com/improve-active-listening-skills/

Institute for Health and Human Potential. (2019). *The meaning of emotional intelligence.* Last Eight Percent. https://www.ihhp.com/meaning-of-emotional-intelligence/

Jackson, J., & Jackson, L. (2015, January 26). *20 statements that communicate empathy to kids.* Connected Families. https://connectedfamilies.org/5-phrases-communicate-empathy-kids/

Jain, R. (2019, March 26). *11 things to say when kids cry.* GoZen! https://gozen.com/11-things-to-say-when-kids-cry/

Johnson, E. (2022, May). *Active listening skills – How to support children with poor listening skills.* Teach Early Years. https://www.teachearlyyears.com/learning-and-development/view/learning-to-listen

Joy, R. (2021, January 25). *EQ vs IQ: How they differ, which is more important?* Healthline. https://www.healthline.com/health/eq-vs-iq

Kadane, L. (2018, October 11). *EQ vs IQ: Why emotional intelligence will take your kid further in life.* Today's Parent. https://www.todaysparent.com/kids/kids-health/eq-vs-iq-why-emotional-intelligence-will-take-kids-farther-in-life/

Katz, L. F., & Gottman, J. M. (1997). Buffering children from marital conflict and dissolution. *Journal of Clinical Child Psychology, 26*(2), 157–171. https://doi.org/10.1207/s15374424jccp2602_4

Kellogg, M. (2022, February 9). *How and why to measure emotional intelligence.* Criteria Corp. https://www.criteriacorp.com/blog/how-and-why-to-measure-emotional-intelligence#:~:text=There%20are%20three%20generally%20accepted

King, E. (2022, June 14). *When it's okay to let your toddler cry.* ILLUMINATION-Curated. https://medium.com/illumination-curated/when-its-okay-to-let-your-toddler-cry-c582a14b7c02

Kristenson, S. (2022, May 2). *Goal setting for kids: 5 steps (with examples).* Develop Good Habits. https://www.developgoodhabits.com/goal-setting-kids/

Lebow, H. I. (2021, June 7). *Emotional intelligence (EQ): Components and tips.* Psych Central. https://psychcentral.com/lib/what-is-emotional-intelligence-eq#components

Lee, A. (2019, August 5). *Self-advocacy: What it is and why it's important.* Understood. https://www.understood.org/en/articles/the-importance-of-self-advocacy

Lee, K. (2019). *How to nurture empathy and emotional intelligence in children.* Verywell Family. https://www.verywellfamily.com/how-to-nurture-empathy-in-kids-and-why-its-so-important-621098

Leyshon, C., & Hamid, M. (2012, September 16). *This week in fiction: Mohsin Hamid.* The New Yorker. https://www.newyorker.com/books/page-turner/this-week-in-fiction-mohsin-hamid

Li, P. (2018a, January 28). *4 types of parenting styles and their effects on the child.* Parenting for Brain. https://www.parentingforbrain.com/4-baumrind-parenting-styles/

Li, P. (2018b, January 28). *What is authoritative parenting? (Examples and comparisons).* Parenting for Brain. https://www.parentingforbrain.com/authoritative-parenting/

Li, P. (2019a, April 13). *Permissive parenting - Why indulgent parenting is bad for your child.* Parenting for Brain. https://www.parentingforbrain.com/permissive-parenting/

Li, P. (2019b, June 27). *Authoritarian parenting (tough love parenting).* Parenting for Brain. https://www.parentingforbrain.com/authoritarian-parenting-tough-love/

Li, P. (2019c, September 15). *6 proven ways to encourage kids effectively (without side effects).* Parenting for Brain. https://www.parentingforbrain.com/words-of-encouragement-for-kids/

Li, P. (2020, October 8). *Uninvolved parenting - Why it's the worst parenting style.* Parenting for Brain. https://www.parentingforbrain.com/uninvolved-parenting/

Li, P. (2021, September 9). *Emotion coaching: How parents can help kids develop self-regulation.* Parenting for Brain. https://www.parentingforbrain.com/emotion-coaching-parents/

Li, P. (2022a, June 30). *Goal setting for kids: 5 simple steps and pitfalls to avoid.* Parenting for Brain.

https://www.parentingforbrain.com/goal-setting-for-kids/

Li, P. (2022b, October 11). *What to do when husband and wife's parenting styles are just too different*. Parenting for Brain. https://www.parentingforbrain.com/parents-dont-agree-on-parenting/

Li, P. (2023, February 4). *What is tiger parenting and is it superior?* Parenting for Brain. https://www.parentingforbrain.com/tiger-parenting/

Lively, S. (2018, September 10). *Why it's okay to let your kids cry*. One Time Through. https://onetimethrough.com/why-its-okay-to-let-your-kids-cry/

Louick, R. (2017, July 2). *How to teach a growth mindset to kids (The 4-week guide)*. Big Life Journal. https://biglifejournal.com/blogs/blog/teach-growth-mindset-kids-activities

Lovering, N. (2022, July 25). *Free-range parenting: The pros and cons*. Psych Central. https://psychcentral.com/blog/do-kids-have-too-much-freedom

Macklin, A. (2022, July 19). Crying: *Is it good or bad? 5 eye-opening facts a parent needs to know*. Good Night Sleep Site. https://goodnightsleepsite.com/2022/07/19/crying-is-it-good-or-bad-5-eye-opening-facts-parent-needs-to-know/

Mangrum, N. (2021, September 8). *Growth mindset for kids – Helping children realize their own potential*. Maryland Teacher Tutors. https://marylandteachertutors.com/growth-mindset-for-kids/

Markham, L. (2023, May 18). *15 ways to raise a child with great values.* Aha! Parenting. https://www.ahaparenting.com/read/values

Mathers, C. (2020, December 1). *10 SMART goals examples for kids.* Develop Good Habits. https://www.developgoodhabits.com/smart-goals-kids/

Matthews, D. (2019, November 1). *Empathy milestones: How your child becomes more empathetic.* Psychology Today. https://www.psychologytoday.com/intl/blog/going-beyond-intelligence/201911/empathy-milestones-how-your-child-becomes-more-empathetic

McCready, A. (2019, December 29). *5 positive parenting techniques you can use in 2020.* Positive Parenting Solutions. https://www.positiveparentingsolutions.com/parenting/positive-parenting-techniques

McFall, S. (2023, February 7). *25 ways to compliment kids to build self-worth.* Prevent Child Abuse Delaware. https://pcadelaware.org/news/2023/1/24/25-ways-to-compliment-kids-to-build-self-worth

Mcilroy, T. (2018, July 13). *17 fun and simple listening activities for kids.* Empowered Parents. https://empoweredparents.co/8-games-to-improve-your-childs-listening-skills/

Mcilroy, T. (2021, April 29). *Why listening skills in early childhood are vital + how to teach them.* Empowered Parents. https://empoweredparents.co/listening-skills-in-early-childhood/

Mentalization. (n.d.). American Psychological Association. https://dictionary.apa.org/mentalization

Merrow, C. (2021, June 15). *Active listening skills for kids.* Empowering Education. https://empoweringeducation.org/blog/active-listening/

Mills, S. (2016, August 11). *What is emotional literacy?* Study.com. https://study.com/academy/lesson/what-is-emotional-literacy.html

Monke, A. (2015, May 8). *5 steps to help kids resolve conflicts.* Sunshine Parenting. https://sunshine-parenting.com/5-steps-to-help-kids-resolve-conflicts/

Monke, A. (2019, November 17). *5 ways to encourage empathy in kids.* Sunshine Parenting. https://sunshine-parenting.com/empathy/

Montgomery, S. (2019, May 21). *8 early signs your child is incredibly emotionally intelligent.* Romper. https://www.romper.com/p/8-early-signs-of-emotional-intelligence-in-toddlers-according-to-experts-17906328

Moravcik Walbert, M. (2021, June 15). *How to understand your child's temperament.* Lifehacker. https://lifehacker.com/how-to-understand-your-childs-temperament-1847091345

Morey, R. (2018, July 16). *How 5 emotionally intelligent CEOs handle their power.* Pagely®. https://pagely.com/blog/emotionally-intelligent-ceos/

Morin, A. (2018). *How to model the behavior you want your child to exhibit.* Verywell Family. https://www.verywellfamily.com/role-model-the-behavior-you-want-to-see-from-your-kids-1094785

Morin, A. (2019, October 16). *How to teach self-advocacy to grade school kids.* Understood. https://www.understood.org/en/articles/6-tips-for-helping-your-grade-schooler-learn-to-self-advocate

Morin, A. (2020, November 21). *How free-range parenting can benefit your child.* Verywell Family. https://www.verywellfamily.com/what-is-free-range-parenting-1095057

Morin, A. (2021a, March 27). *6 parenting strategies for raising emotionally intelligent kids.* Verywell Family. https://www.verywellfamily.com/tips-for-raising-an-emotionally-intelligent-child-4157946

Morin, A. (2021b, March 27). *The difference between punishment and discipline.* Verywell Family. https://www.verywellfamily.com/the-difference-between-punishment-and-discipline-1095044

Morin, A. (2022, August 9). *4 types of parenting styles and their effects on kids.* Verywell Family. https://www.verywellfamily.com/types-of-parenting-styles-1095045

Muriel, C. (2022, May 8). *20 fun conflict resolution activities for kids (printable PDF): Worksheets, games and activities.* Very Special Tales. https://veryspecialtales.com/conflict-resolution-activities-for-kids-pdf/

Muriel, C. (2023, January 30). *28 fun emotional intelligence activities for kids.* Very Special Tales. https://veryspecialtales.com/emotional-intelligence-activities-for-kids/

Myriam, I. (2020, December 2). *Discover and nurture your child's talents in 5 steps.* Kiddy123.

https://www.kiddy123.com/article/discover-and-nurture-your-childs-talents-in-5-steps.html

Naik, A. (2023, March 1). *Examples of goals for children (In the short & long term).* GoHenry. https://www.gohenry.com/uk/blog/family/examples-of-goals-for-children

Nieman, E. (2020, September 10). *15 activities to build good listening skills.* Kids Activities Blog. https://kidsactivitiesblog.com/52641/listening-skills/

O'Brien Martin, C. (2021, September 4). *How to teach self-awareness skills to children.* WholeChildCounseling. https://www.wholechildcounseling.com/post/how-to-teach-self-awareness-skills-to-children

Ocampo, M. (2021, August 30). *Why supporting your child's self awareness is critical.* Opal Academy. https://www.opal-academy.com/blog/why-supporting-your-child-s-self-awareness-is-critical-in-the-early-years

Ockwell-Smith, S. (2015, January 13). *Why it's OK to let your baby or child cry (sometimes).* Sarah Ockwell-Smith. https://sarahockwell-smith.com/2015/01/13/why-its-ok-to-let-your-baby-or-child-cry-sometimes/

Parlakian, R. (2016, February 1). *How to help your child develop empathy.* Zero to Three. https://www.zerotothree.org/resource/how-to-help-your-child-develop-empathy/

Parlakian, R. (2020, November 10). *Managing emotions as parents.* PBS KIDS for Parents. https://www.pbs.org/parents/thrive/managing-emotions-as-parents

Patel, R. B. (2020, May 20). *11 positive parenting tips every parent should know.* Our Children. https://ptaourchildren.org/11-positive-parenting-tips/

Patino, E. (2019, August 5). *Build self-awareness in grade school | Tips to make kids self-aware.* Understood. https://www.understood.org/en/articles/5-ways-to-help-your-grade-schooler-gain-self-awareness

Pearson, C. (2020, July 13). *5 questions to gauge kids' emotional intelligence — and help them boost it.* HuffPost. https://www.huffpost.com/entry/questions-gauge-kids-emotional-intelligence-help-boost_l_5f08722cc5b63a72c340bb66

Phillips, H. (2019). *What are the biggest problems with helicopter parents?* Verywell Family. https://www.verywellfamily.com/helicopter-parents-do-they-help-or-hurt-kids-1095041

Pinkowitz, S. (2012, October 4). *What are self-awareness skills?* LearningWorks for Kids. https://learningworksforkids.com/skills/self-awareness/

Pittard, M. (2023, June 27). *7 ways to teach your child to self-advocate.* Beaming Health. https://beaminghealth.com/article/7-ways-to-teach-your-child-to-self-advocate

Plant, R. (2021, July 30). *What is tiger parenting?* Verywell Family. https://www.verywellfamily.com/what-is-tiger-parenting-5188954

Plant, R. (2022, November 29). *What is gentle parenting?* Verywell Family. https://www.verywellfamily.com/what-is-gentle-parenting-5189566#:~:text=Gentle%20parenting%20is%20an%20evidence

Positive Action Staff. (2020, August 7). *Teaching self-awareness to students: 5 effective activities.* Positive Action. https://www.positiveaction.net/blog/teaching-self-awareness-to-students

Raising Children Network (Australia). (2022a, October 18). *Understanding and managing emotions: Children and teenagers.* Raising Children Network. https://raisingchildren.net.au/preschoolers/development/preschoolers-social-emotional-development/understanding-managing-emotions-children-teenagers#:~:text=down%20and%20cope.-

Raising Children Network (Australia). (2022b, October 26). *Crying: Children 1-8 years.* Raising Children Network. https://raisingchildren.net.au/toddlers/behaviour/crying-tantrums/crying-children-1-8-years

Reddy, C. (2016, May 1). *Emotional intelligence: How to measure and assess.* Wisestep. https://content.wisestep.com/emotional-intelligence-measure-assess/

Ross, J. (2016). *Self-advocacy: Strategies for all ages.* Smart Kids. https://www.smartkidswithld.org/getting-help/raising-independent-kids/self-advocacy-strategies-ages/

Ryann, A. (2020a). *7 attributes kids need to build resilience & overcome challenges.* Raising Kids with Purpose. https://raisingkidswithpurpose.com/build-resilience-to-overcome-challenges/

Ryann, A. (2020b, January 23). *7 ways to help kids develop self-awareness skills (that also help with kindness & empathy!).* Raising Kids with Purpose. https://raisingkidswithpurpose.com/self-awareness-skills-for-kids/

Rymanowicz, K. (2018, November 1). *Teaching children to be their own self-advocate*. Early Childhood Development. https://www.canr.msu.edu/news/teaching-children-to-be-their-own-self-advocate

Sanvictores, T., & Mendez, M. D. (2022). *Types of Parenting Styles and Effects On Children*. In StatPearls. StatPearls Publishing.

Sauber Millacci, T. (2019, February 8). *19+ innovative ways to teach emotional intelligence to kids*. PositivePsychology.com. https://positivepsychology.com/emotional-intelligence-for-kids/

Sauber Millacci, T. (2021, December 29). *How to nurture a growth mindset in kids: 8 best activities*. PositivePsychology.com. https://positivepsychology.com/growth-mindset-for-kids/

Schreiner, K., & Falardeau, C. (2020, July 8). *Parent education: Parenting to promote self-advocacy*. Foothills Academy. https://www.foothillsacademy.org/community/articles/support-self-advocacy

Segal, J., Smith, M., Robinson, L., & Shubin, J. (2021, July). *Improving emotional intelligence (EQ)*. HelpGuide. https://www.helpguide.org/articles/mental-health/emotional-intelligence-eq.htm#:~:text=Emotional%20intelligence%20helps%20you%20build

Shaik, K. (2022, February 16). *Why emotional intelligence is more important than IQ*. LinkedIn. https://www.linkedin.com/pulse/why-emotional-intelligence-more-important-than-iq-khaleel-shaik

Shenfield, T. (2020, February 8). *How to effectively manage your emotions and become a better parent*. Advanced Psychology

Services. https://www.psy-ed.com/wpblog/manage-your-emotions/

Short and long term goals for children. (2022, January 17). NumberWorks'nWords. https://numberworksnwords.com/global/blog/short-and-long-term-goals-for-children/#.ZGqh6-xBxAc

Silm, T. (2013). *Positive discipline: Punishment vs. discipline.* Michigan State University. https://www.canr.msu.edu/news/positive_discipline_p unishment_vs_discipline

Silver, C. (2022, December 4). *How to parent with a partner when you can't agree on a parenting style.* Parents. https://www.parents.com/parenting/better-parenting/how-to-parent-with-a-partner-when-you-cant-agree-on-a-parenting-style/

Singhal, M. (2021, January 3). *6 things emotionally intelligent parents do differently.* Psychology Today. https://www.psychologytoday.com/intl/blog/the-therapist-mommy/202101/6-things-emotionally-intelligent-parents-do-differently#:~:text=Emotionally%20Intelligent%20par ents%20don

Slayback, Z., Coleman, T. K., Nelson, C., & Morehouse, I. (2015). *Freedom without permission: How to live free in a world that isn't.* Createspace Independent Publishing Platform.

Soderlund, A. (2017, October 23). *7 science-backed ways to teach your child self-regulation.* Nurture and Thrive. https://nurtureandthriveblog.com/how-to-teach-your-child-self-regulation/

Soderlund, A. (2018, March 20). *Be your child's emotion-coach with these 10 powerful parenting phrases.* Nurture and Thrive.

https://nurtureandthriveblog.com/emotion-coaching-parents/

Staake, J. (2023, January 27). *20 growth mindset activities to inspire confidence in kids.* We Are Teachers. https://www.weareteachers.com/growth-mindset/

Steed, A. (2022, November 8). *Emotion coaching: Helping parents bring out the best in their kids.* Relationships Australia. https://www.relationshipsnsw.org.au/blog/emotion-coaching-for-parents/

Stocks, W. (2016, November 30). *Using a feelings wheel to name and understand emotions.* Hope 4 Hurting Kids. https://hope4hurtingkids.com/emotions/understanding-emotions/feelings-wheel-name-understand-emotions/

Surbhi, S. (2016, April 16). *Difference between IQ and EQ (with comparison chart).* Key Differences. https://keydifferences.com/difference-between-iq-and-eq.html

Suttie, J. (2016, June 10). *Seven ways to foster empathy in kids.* Greater Good Magazine. https://greatergood.berkeley.edu/article/item/seven_ways_to_foster_empathy_in_kids

66 journal prompts for kids for self reflection. (2021, November 8). Mål Paper. https://malpaper.com/blogs/news/66-journal-prompts-for-kids-for-self-reflection

Talaris Institute. (2023). *Five steps of emotion coaching.* Parenting Counts. https://www.parentingcounts.org/five-steps-of-emotion-coaching/

Tapp, F. (2022, December 16). *30 journal prompts for kids to aid self-discovery.* Parents.

https://www.parents.com/kids/education/30-journal-prompts-for-kids-to-aid-self-discovery/

Tarr, K. (2022, July 14). *Emotion coaching 101: What it is and why kids need it.* Parenting Place. https://parentingplace.nz/resources/emotion-coaching-101-what-it-is-and-why-kids-need-it

Taylor, M. (2019, January 6). *Emotional intelligence activities for kids.* Imagination Soup. https://imaginationsoup.net/emotional-intelligence-activities-kids/

Teaching kids to be self-aware. (2019, September 1). The Pathway 2 Success. https://www.thepathway2success.com/teaching-kids-to-be-self-aware-2/

Thorp, T. (2016, April 15). *How to use meditation to visualize your goals.* Chopra. https://chopra.com/articles/how-to-use-meditation-to-visualize-your-goals#:~:text=Try%20the%20following

10 ways to teach your children to overcome obstacles. (2010, May 24). All pro Dad. https://www.allprodad.com/10-ways-teach-children-overcome-obstacles/

10 ways to unleash your child's talents. (2018, September 4). Kids Academy. https://www.kidsacademy.mobi/storytime/how-to-discover-your-childs-talent/

10+ self-awareness activities for kids. (2021, October 19). The Pathway 2 Success. https://www.thepathway2success.com/10-self-awareness-activities-for-kids/

12 self-regulation strategies for young children. (2021, January 24). Heart-Mind Online. https://heartmindonline.org/resources/12-self-regulation-strategies-for-young-children

University of California Davis Health. (2023, February 21). *The power of positive parenting.* UC Davis Health Children's Hospital. https://health.ucdavis.edu/children/patient-education/Positive-Parenting#:~:text=What%20is%20positive%20parenting%20and

University of California Santa Cruz. (2022, March 7). *What is self-advocacy?* UC Santa Cruz Disability Resource Center. https://drc.ucsc.edu/general-resources/resources/online-resources/self-advocacy.html#:~:text=

Vadi, D. L., & Jacobson, M. L. (2020, January 13). *Behind every young child who believes in himself is a parent who believed first. - Matthew Jacobson.* 365 Quotes. https://365quotes.in/behind-every-young-child-who-believes-in-himself-is-a-parent-who-believed-first-matthew-jacobson/

Waldman, M. (2022a, March 14). *Teaching emotions to young children: Tips and tricks.* HiMama Blog - Resources for Daycare Centers. https://www.himama.com/blog/teaching-emotions-to-young-children-tips-and-tricks/#:~:text=The%20number%20one%20tool%20we

Waldman, M. (2022b, March 29). *The importance of emotional intelligence in young learners.* HiMama Blog - Resources for Daycare Centers. https://www.himama.com/blog/the-importance-of-emotional-intelligence-in-young-learners/

Walsh, E., & Walsh, D. (2019, May 9). *How children develop empathy.* Psychology Today. https://www.psychologytoday.com/us/blog/smart-parenting-smarter-kids/201905/how-children-develop-empathy#:~:text=Empathy%20means%20that%20a%20child

Walters Wright, L. (2019, August 5). *Communication skills | 10 ways to help your grade school child.* Understood. https://www.understood.org/en/articles/10-ways-to-improve-your-grade-schoolers-communication-skills

Wartski, S. (2020, August 10). *Is your kid emotionally intelligent? A psychologist shares the traits to look for—and how to teach them.* CNBC Make It. https://www.cnbc.com/2020/08/10/is-your-kid-emotionally-intelligent-psychologist-how-to-raise-high-eq-children.html

Welch, S. (2018, May 17). *Important values to teach your child by 5 years old.* Shepherds Friendly. https://www.shepherdsfriendly.co.uk/resources/important-values-teach-child-age-5/

Wellness Team. (2022, August 22). *How to improve your child's self-awareness.* Healthy Mummy Wellness. https://healthymummywellness.com/how-to-improve-your-childs-self-awareness/

What are the basic emotions in children? (2018, November 5). You Are Mom. https://youaremom.com/children/basic-emotions-in-children/

What is active listening? (2023). Twinkl. https://www.twinkl.com.ph/teaching-wiki/active-listening

What is mentalizing? (2016, November 9). MBT-TBM Canada. https://mbt-tbm.org/what-mentalizing

What is self-advocacy? (2022, November 10). Communication Community. https://www.communicationcommunity.com/what-is-self-advocacy/

Why teaching children empathy is more important than ever. (2018, February 22). Goodstart Early Learning. https://www.goodstart.org.au/parenting/why-teaching-children-empathy-is-more-important-than-ever

Wildenberg, L. (2017, May 22). *20 questions to assess your child's emotional quotient (EQ part 1).* Lori Wildenberg. https://loriwildenberg.com/2017/05/22/20-questions-to-assess-your-childs-emotional-quotient-eq-part-1/

Williams, E. (2018, May 29). *What is a growth mindset and why it matters for children and their parents.* Third Space Learning. https://thirdspacelearning.com/blog/what-is-growth-mindset/

Williamson, N. (2021, May 20). *How to explain and teach empathy to a child.* As They Grow. https://www.as-they-grow.com/how-to-explain-and-teach-empathy-to-a-child

Williamson, T. (2021, January 26). *101 compliments for kids that'll raise them up!* Mindfulmazing. https://www.mindfulmazing.com/101-compliments-for-kids/

Wirth, J. (2023, April 9). *35 positive affirmations to empower your child.* Parents. https://www.parents.com/kids/health/childrens-mental-health/32positive-affirmations-for-kids-and-why-theyre-so-important/

Yacoub, A. (2021, September 30). *How to teach your child a growth mindset.* TherapyWorks. https://therapyworks.com/blog/language-development/home-tips/growth-mindset/

Zapata, K. (2022, October 20). *What is gentle parenting?* Parents. https://www.parents.com/parenting/better-parenting/style/what-is-gentle-parenting/

Zeltser, F. (2021). *A psychologist shares the 4 styles of parenting—and the type that researchers say is the most successful.* CNBC Make It. https://www.cnbc.com/2021/06/29/child-psychologist-explains-4-types-of-parenting-and-how-to-tell-which-is-right-for-you.html